# Welcome to the EVERYTHING® series!

THESE HANDY, accessible books give you all you need to tackle a difficult project, gain a new hobby, comprehend a fascinating topic, prepare for an exam, or even brush up on something you learned back in school but have since forgotten.

You can read an EVERYTHING® book from cover to cover or just pick out the information you want from our four useful boxes: e-facts, e-ssentials, e-alerts, and e-questions. We literally give you everything you need to know on the subject, but throw in a lot of fun stuff along the way, too.

We now have well over 300 EVERYTHING® books in print, spanning such wide-ranging topics as weddings, pregnancy, wine, music, one-pot cooking, managing people, and so much more. When you're done reading them all, you can finally say you know EVERYTHING®!

**Ⓔ Facts:** Important sound bytes of information

**Ⓔ Essentials:** Quick and handy tips

**Ⓔ Alerts!:** Urgent warnings

**Ⓔ Questions?:** Solutions to common problems

THE

# EVERYTHING®
— Series —

Dear Reader,

My daughter, Laurel, was an easy baby to get to sleep at night, a baby who gave me only a few bad nights of floor-pacing (me), screaming (her), and crying (both of us). As I talked to other parents, though, I learned that many others had a much tougher time of it. The parents who told me these stories were often at their wits' end. Not only were they concerned about their babies not getting enough sleep, but they were also concerned about themselves. It's tough to parent well or work well on three hours' sleep.

In the years since then, I've become an author and getting your baby to sleep is clearly a topic of wide interest. You don't have to be a researcher to figure that out—just a mom who's exchanged horror stories with other moms.

So for all parents out there whose babies won't go to sleep, or stay asleep, or have other sleep-related problems, I've written a book that I hope will help.

From now on, when you say "Good night" to your little one, you can mean it. It will be a good night!

Cynthia MacGregor

THE

# EVERYTHING®

## GET YOUR
## BABY TO SLEEP
# BOOK

Solve common problems
so you can rest, too

Cynthia MacGregor

Avon, Massachusetts

*Dedication*
To my daughter, Laurel, now grown and a mother
herself, and to the memory of my mother, Yvonne.

• • •

Copyright ©2005, F+W Publications, Inc.
All rights reserved. This book, or parts thereof, may not be reproduced
in any form without permission from the publisher; exceptions
are made for brief excerpts used in published reviews.

An Everything® Series Book.
Everything® and everything.com® are registered
trademarks of F+W Publications, Inc.

Published by Adams Media, an F+W Publications Company
57 Littlefield Street, Avon, MA 02322 U.S.A.
*www.adamsmedia.com*

ISBN: 1-59337-356-2

Printed in Canada.

J   I   H   G   F   E   D   C   B   A

**Library of Congress Cataloging-in-Publication Data**
MacGregor, Cynthia.
The everything get your baby to sleep book / Cynthia Macgregor.
p.       cm. — (An everything series book)
ISBN 1-59337-356-2
1. Infants—Sleep. 2. Infants—Care. 3. Sleep disorders in
children. I. Title. II. Series: Everything series.
RJ506.S55M33 2005
649'.122—dc22
2005011006

*This book is available at quantity discounts for bulk purchases.
For information, please call 1-800-872-5627.*

THE

# EVERYTHING

## Series

## EDITORIAL

Publishing Director: Gary M. Krebs
Managing Editor: Kate McBride
Copy Chief: Laura M. Daly
Acquisitions Editor: Kate Burgo
Development Editor: Karen Johnson Jacot
Production Editor: Jamie Wielgus

## PRODUCTION

Director of Manufacturing & Technology: Susan Beale
Associate Director of Production: Michelle Roy Kelly
Cover Design: Paul Beatrice and Matt LeBlanc
Layout and Graphics:
Colleen Cunningham, Holly Curtis,
Erin Dawson, Sorae Lee

*Visit the entire Everything® series at www.everything.com*

## Acknowledgments

I couldn't have written this without the help of a dear friend and very talented writer. Huge thanks to Jesse Leaf.

# *Contents*

Top Ten Baby Sleep Questions You
Can Solve after Reading This Book . . . . . . . . . . . . . xii

Introduction . . . . . . . . . . . . . . . . . . . . . . . . . . . . . . xiii

Chapter 1: *A Good Night's Sleep . . . for All* . . . . . . 1
The Importance of Sleep . . . . . . . . . . . . . . . . . . . . . . . . 2
Your Baby's Sleep Needs . . . . . . . . . . . . . . . . . . . . . . . . 3
Sleep Patterns and REM Sleep . . . . . . . . . . . . . . . . . . . . . 5
Sleeping Through the Night . . . . . . . . . . . . . . . . . . . . . . 10
A Noise in the Night . . . . . . . . . . . . . . . . . . . . . . . . . . 13
You Can't Fool Mother Nature . . . . . . . . . . . . . . . . . . . . 14

Chapter 2: *What's Keeping Baby Awake? Hunger,
Schedules, and Pain* . . . . . . . . . . . . . . . . . . . . . . . . 17
The Number One Internal Problem—Hunger . . . . . . . . . . 18
On-Demand Feeding versus Scheduled Feeding . . . . . . . . 21
A Happy Trade-Off . . . . . . . . . . . . . . . . . . . . . . . . . . . 24
When Your Baby's Schedule Doesn't Mesh with Yours . . . 25
Colic: Frequent Scapegoat, Real Pain . . . . . . . . . . . . . . . 27
Teething . . . . . . . . . . . . . . . . . . . . . . . . . . . . . . . . . . 29
Intestinal Distress . . . . . . . . . . . . . . . . . . . . . . . . . . . 30

Chapter 3: *Other Things Keeping Baby Awake* . . 33
Food Isn't Always the Answer . . . . . . . . . . . . . . . . . . . . 34

Anxieties . . . . . . . . . . . . . . . . . . . . . . . . . . . . . . . . . . . .35

Wide Awake in the Evening. . . . . . . . . . . . . . . . . . . . . . .36

Bad Dreams and Nightmares. . . . . . . . . . . . . . . . . . . . . .37

Myclonic Jerks. . . . . . . . . . . . . . . . . . . . . . . . . . . . . . . .43

Sleep Apnea. . . . . . . . . . . . . . . . . . . . . . . . . . . . . . . . . .44

Other Sleep-Disturbing Breathing Problems . . . . . . . . . .46

External Problems. . . . . . . . . . . . . . . . . . . . . . . . . . . . . .49


CHAPTER 4: *Signal When Ready* . . . . . . . . . . . . . . .53

Early Cycles . . . . . . . . . . . . . . . . . . . . . . . . . . . . . . . . . .54

Do Routines Matter? . . . . . . . . . . . . . . . . . . . . . . . . . . . .54

Signs That Baby Is Ready for Bed . . . . . . . . . . . . . . . . . .55

Establish Regular Sleep Habits and Routines . . . . . . . . .56

Settling Baby into His Crib . . . . . . . . . . . . . . . . . . . . . . .62

Recognizing Night and Day . . . . . . . . . . . . . . . . . . . . . .64

When Baby Is Overtired . . . . . . . . . . . . . . . . . . . . . . . . .66

Teaching Baby to Get Herself Back to Sleep . . . . . . . . . .67


CHAPTER 5: *Soothing Baby to Sleep* . . . . . . . . . . .75

Calming Your Crying Baby. . . . . . . . . . . . . . . . . . . . . . . .76

Rocking and Soothing Motion Techniques . . . . . . . . . . .77

Singing and Talking . . . . . . . . . . . . . . . . . . . . . . . . . . . .82

A Cry for Attention . . . . . . . . . . . . . . . . . . . . . . . . . . . . .84

Swaddling. . . . . . . . . . . . . . . . . . . . . . . . . . . . . . . . . . . .84

Massage . . . . . . . . . . . . . . . . . . . . . . . . . . . . . . . . . . . . .86

Quiet Games . . . . . . . . . . . . . . . . . . . . . . . . . . . . . . . . . .87

Tactics to Avoid . . . . . . . . . . . . . . . . . . . . . . . . . . . . . . . .88

CHAPTER 6: **Sound and Light** . . . . . . . . . . . . . . . . . . 91

How Babies React to Sound . . . . . . . . . . . . . . . . . . . . . . . .92

Getting Baby Used to Distractions . . . . . . . . . . . . . . . . . .94

Naptime Is for Learning . . . . . . . . . . . . . . . . . . . . . . . . . .96

Quiet versus Loud . . . . . . . . . . . . . . . . . . . . . . . . . . . . . . .99

Dark versus Light . . . . . . . . . . . . . . . . . . . . . . . . . . . . . . .100

Using Sound Machines . . . . . . . . . . . . . . . . . . . . . . . . . . .102


CHAPTER 7: **The Proper Nursery** . . . . . . . . . . . . . . 107

Choosing the Right Crib . . . . . . . . . . . . . . . . . . . . . . . . . .108

Choosing a Cradle . . . . . . . . . . . . . . . . . . . . . . . . . . . . . . .112

Taking Safety Precautions . . . . . . . . . . . . . . . . . . . . . . . .113

Be Aware of Hazards . . . . . . . . . . . . . . . . . . . . . . . . . . . . .116

Bedding . . . . . . . . . . . . . . . . . . . . . . . . . . . . . . . . . . . . . . .117

Get the Right Clothes for Sleeping . . . . . . . . . . . . . . . . . .120

Other Suffocation Hazards . . . . . . . . . . . . . . . . . . . . . . . .120

SIDS . . . . . . . . . . . . . . . . . . . . . . . . . . . . . . . . . . . . . . . . .121

Baby's Own Room . . . . . . . . . . . . . . . . . . . . . . . . . . . . . . .124


CHAPTER 8: **The Family Bed** . . . . . . . . . . . . . . . . . 125

Parents and Baby Sharing a Room . . . . . . . . . . . . . . . . . .126

Parents and Baby Sharing a Bed . . . . . . . . . . . . . . . . . . . .127

Cosleeping and Nursing . . . . . . . . . . . . . . . . . . . . . . . . . .129

Disadvantages of Cosleeping . . . . . . . . . . . . . . . . . . . . . .130

Cosleeping and Safety . . . . . . . . . . . . . . . . . . . . . . . . . . . .133

Privacy Aspects for Parents . . . . . . . . . . . . . . . . . . . . . . .139

Moving Baby Out of Your Bed . . . . . . . . . . . . . . . . . . . . .140

CHAPTER 9: *Adjusting to New Surroundings* .... 143

Changes at Home ................................. 144

Moving Baby to Her Own Room .................... 147

Changes When Traveling ......................... 149

Visiting Relatives in Their Home ................. 154

Sleeping in the Car ............................. 158

Day Care ...................................... 160

Sickness and Health ............................ 162

Honor His Fears—Within Reason ................. 164


CHAPTER 10: *Naptime* ........................ 167

The Benefits of Napping ......................... 168

How Long and How Many? ....................... 170

How Naptime Differs from Nighttime .............. 171

Establishing Naptimes and Feeding Times .......... 173

Promoting Good Nap Habits ...................... 175

Napping Problems ............................... 178

No Substitute for Nighttime Sleep ................ 180


CHAPTER 11: *Good Morning!* .................. 183

Babies Who Wake Up Groggy ..................... 184

Handling a Groggy Baby ......................... 186

Babies Who Are Early Risers ..................... 188

When Baby Is Wide Awake ....................... 189

Subtle Methods for Waking Up Baby .............. 192

CHAPTER 12: *Making Up for Lost Time . . .*
*and Sleep (Yours)*. . . . . . . . . . . . . . . . . . . . . . . . . 195

Coping When Baby Won't Sleep . . . . . . . . . . . . . . . . . . . 196

Crying It Out. . . . . . . . . . . . . . . . . . . . . . . . . . . . . . . . . .200

Finding Support Through Family, Friends, and
    Babysitters . . . . . . . . . . . . . . . . . . . . . . . . . . . . . . . .203

Don't Blame Yourself . . . or Anyone Else . . . . . . . . . . . .206


APPENDIX A: *Additional Resources* . . . . . . . . . . . 209

APPENDIX B: *Support Groups*. . . . . . . . . . . . . . . . 213


INDEX . . . . . . . . . . . . . . . . . . . . . . . . . . . . . . . . . . . . . .215

## Top Ten Baby Sleep Questions You Can Solve after Reading This Book

1. How do I get my child to sleep at night?

2. How do I get him to sleep through the night?

3. Why does she seem to stop breathing sometimes when she sleeps?

4. How can I cope? I've had only two hours' sleep!

5. How do I get my baby to nap?

6. My baby moves around and makes noises in her sleep. Is she getting a good rest?

7. My baby sleeps more in the daytime than at night. What do I do?

8. How can I tell when my baby is ready to go to sleep?

9. Which is better—to keep him on a routine or to put him to bed when he seems tired?

10. If she wakes up during the night and she was fed only an hour ago, should I give her a bottle to help her get back to sleep?

# Introduction

WHEN YOU SAY "GOOD NIGHT" to your baby, do you say it through clenched teeth, knowing the night is going to be anything but good? Has getting your baby to sleep for the night become a major struggle or a complicated routine? Is the middle of the night in your household a torture of interrupted sleep, hours spent with a crying baby, or at best an awake baby, placid but definitely not sleeping? Is your baby's sleep schedule radically impairing your own, preventing you from getting anything close to your full complement of sleep? Are your eyes red and your nerves frayed? Are you and your spouse dragging your way through the days, suffering from a serious sleep deficit and wondering when it will end?

It ends now with this book. It ends with you learning techniques and plans for getting your baby to go to sleep at night when you want him to, without your having to drive him around and around the block in your car, stay in his room with him for two hours, or go through any other complex routine. Of course, if he's very young, he'll still wake up for feedings during the night at first, but he'll soon learn how to go back to sleep once he's full, instead of remaining awake. With the aid of this book, you'll learn how to help him get himself back to sleep when he wakes up for any reason.

Naps are important, too. Though they don't replace nighttime sleep, they're a key element in your baby's good health and well-being, as well as for his disposition. Some babies go to sleep readily at night but are less successful at napping. Sometimes parents have unrealistic expectations for how often their baby sleeps; newborns do not sleep around the clock and wake up only for feedings. Right from the start, they have periods of wakefulness and periods of sleep.

The trick is in getting them to sleep when you want them to. Fortunately, this isn't "The Impossible Dream." Do you want to know how to get your baby to go to sleep at a regular time each night, sleep well during the night, and nap sufficiently for her needs? Note that I didn't say "sleep through the night." This is a misnomer. Babies don't literally sleep through the night any more than anyone else does. We all wake up at times during the night, but in most cases we roll over, settle down, go right back to sleep, and in all likelihood don't even remember the episode in the morning. Your baby can do the same. Do you want to help your baby to sleep well and get the rest he needs and help insure that the rest of your family also has a good night's sleep as a result?

Read on! We are going to take a path that works with Mother Nature and Mother You. Science has come a long way in understanding how and why your baby does what she does, and *The Everything® Get Your Baby to Sleep Book* uses this information to guide you and your baby to a good night's sleep.

## Chapter 1

# A Good Night's Sleep . . . for All

The fact that sleep is important is indisputable. Sleep is necessary for the body to rest and restore itself, for growth, and for mental well-being and clear thinking. But when there's a new baby in the house, not only may he or she not sleep well, but the sleep of everyone else in the house is usually disturbed as well.

## The Importance of Sleep

You want your baby to sleep well for all the obvious reasons . . . for his sake and for your own, as well as for the sake of everyone else in your household. A tired baby is a cranky baby, and a tired mom or dad is often cranky, too. An older sibling whose sleep has been disturbed for several nights is a child who not only may well become cranky, but is also more likely to become susceptible to germs that are floating around.

Sleep is just as necessary as food or drink for a person's well-being. Without food and fluids, our bodies cannot function, cannot grow, and cannot survive. But sleep is just as important. It's essential for a person's good health (both physical and mental), and this is true for people of all ages, including newborns and other babies. But unfortunately, babies don't always sleep as well as parents would like. When your baby is awake at night and crying, nobody in the house can get any sleep—the very thing that everyone needs the most.

Ⓔ **Fact**

A typical newborn baby spends 16½ hours of the day asleep. By the time he's eighteen months old, he's sleeping 13½ hours every day. However, this is only an average, and if your baby sleeps for more or less time than that, as long as your child is growing and developing normally, there is no need to worry about it.

Sleep is a big mystery. Though science understands the physical mechanisms of sleep, it does not understand the ways in which sleep works to restore the body's strength, the mind's ease, or the body's overall well-being. Nonetheless, nobody questions the need for sleep.

When adults fail to get adequate sleep, the mind and body step in and take a stand. The person may find themselves falling asleep at their desk at work, while driving a car, or at some other unfortunate or dangerous time and place. There are other ways, too, in which the body may display the effects of getting insufficient sleep. Some of the symptoms of sleep deprivation in adults include:

- Having difficulty in thinking or thinking clearly
- Feeling cross and cranky
- Experiencing a lack of energy
- Making bad decisions
- Losing your appetite
- Becoming impatient

## Your Baby's Sleep Needs

Children, including babies, need sleep just as much as adults do, if not more. Though some of the effects of sleep deprivation in adults are either not relevant to or not observable in infants, some are—especially crankiness. A cranky baby is no joy to be around! The fact that the mom and dad may be cranky themselves, due to their own sleep deprivation if the baby had them up all night, only exacerbates an already bad situation.

You know your baby needs plenty of sleep to grow and be healthy and happy, and you want him to get a good night's sleep, rather than sleeping all day. Unfortunately, babies don't come equipped with "sleep" buttons or on/off switches. Getting a baby to sleep isn't as easy as turning off a stereo or putting your computer into "sleep" mode.

## Ⓔ *Fact*

Your baby may well be sleeping through the night by age six months at the latest. If he isn't and it is causing a problem for you and if none of the solutions in this book works for you, then discuss the situation with your pediatrician to see if there is a medical problem that's causing the situation.

Fortunately, however, there are things you can do to help your baby get the rest she needs and help the rest of your family have a peaceful night's sleep at the same time. You need to be prepared for the possibility that your baby's first few nights or even her first few weeks will include more wakeful time than you would like. In one recent study, researchers observed newborn babies to find out just how many hours per day they slept. Babies in the study slept an average of two-thirds of the time, about sixteen hours per day. Yet, that is merely an average. Some babies in the study slept as little as nine hours per day; while at the other extreme, some slept for twenty-one hours.

What is the average sleep requirement for a baby?

- *One week old:* a bit over 16 hours per day, of which half is nighttime sleep and half is daytime sleep
- *Three months old:* around 14½ hours per day
- *One year old:* a bit under 14 hours per day
- Eighteen months old: around 13½ hours per day

But again, these are average or typical figures. If your child sleeps more or fewer hours, that doesn't mean he is unhealthy or displaying troublesome patterns. It doesn't necessarily mean anything is wrong.

By the age of six weeks, your baby's body should recognize night from day, with the baby sleeping more during the nighttime hours than during the daytime hours. As she gets older, her sleep will become more consolidated: She will sleep for longer stretches at a time at night and she will remain awake for longer stretches at a time during the day.

## Sleep Patterns and REM Sleep

Our sleep patterns can be broken into two basic types: REM sleep and non-REM sleep. REM is an acronym for Rapid Eye Movement. During REM sleep, a person's eyeballs move around rapidly, perhaps because they are "looking at" the people or things they are dreaming about.

In babies, it is not only the eyeballs that are active during REM sleep. In fact, when talking about infants, the terminology used for the two types of sleep is often "active sleep" (REM) and "quiet sleep" (non-REM). Babies in active sleep may move their arms and/or their legs in addition to their eyes. They may also coo or make other noises. This is in a way equivalent to talking in their sleep. Their eyes may even be partly open. This does not indicate that they are not sleeping. It also does not indicate that they are experiencing a tummy ache or other discomfort. It does not signify a problem.

## Ⓔ *Question?*

**My baby is very active during part of the night when she is sleeping. Does this prevent her from getting the rest she needs?**
No, a baby who experiences "active sleep" is still getting the degree of sleep and amount of rest that she needs. Even if she coos, whimpers, or moves her body or limbs and even if her eyes are partly open, she is still getting a good night's sleep.

According to Richard Ferber, M.D., author of *Solve Your Child's Sleep Problems*, unborn babies develop sleep patterns while still in the uterus. By the sixth or seventh month of your pregnancy, your baby is capable of REM sleep and soon thereafter begins to experience non-REM sleep. A newborn baby, on falling asleep, immediately enters the REM sleep phase, or active sleep. At around three months old, the baby will first enter non-REM sleep, or quiet sleep, when she falls asleep and will maintain this pattern from then on throughout her lifetime.

The proportion of time a baby spends in REM sleep, as opposed to non-REM sleep, is greater than it is in adults or even in older children. The reason for this is one of life's mysteries, but it's nonetheless a fact. As the baby grows older, he'll spend proportionately more time in non-REM, or quiet, sleep, and less time in REM, or active, sleep.

## Ⓔ *Alert!*

Because you want your baby to learn that nighttime is for sleeping and that daytime is for being awake, it's useful to put your baby to sleep in a darkened room at night. If his crib is in your room for the first few months, keep the lights low while your baby is asleep, even when you're in the room. If his crib is in a room he shares with a sibling, try to keep the lights as low as is practical when the older child is still awake and the baby is supposed to be sleeping.

### Sleep Patterns in Babies

A baby's sleep pattern early in life typically involves from two to four hours of sleep at a time, followed by a period of wakefulness, a pattern that may recur around the clock with no regard to whether it's day or night. Your baby has spent the first nine months of her existence in your uterus, where it is always dark, and it will take her a while to associate light with activity and with being awake and alert to what's going on around her.

Differences in sleep patterns among adults are very normal. The same is true among babies. Though certain patterns are average, a deviation from that pattern is usually still quite normal.

Babies are individuals. Just as babies begin to demonstrate a rudimentary but recognizable personality at an early age ("She's a happy baby," "He's a fussy baby," "She's a placid baby," "He's so alert and interested!"), they also show their recognizable differences, one from the other, in other ways, and one of these is in sleep patterns. So if you know someone with a baby the same age as yours who sleeps more, or less, or simply at different hours, don't worry about it. We're all different . . . babies, too.

### Ⓔ Fact

The first six weeks are frequently the toughest for the parents, as it is around the age of six weeks that your baby is most likely to begin differentiating day from night, sleeping longer during the nighttime while remaining awake for longer stretches during the day. Please do not be alarmed if this transition takes place earlier or later in your baby. Such variations are quite normal.

New parents tend to worry that their children aren't eating enough, sleeping enough, or reaching the various developmental stages soon enough. "Is she normal?" "Is he all right?" The fact is that most babies sleep enough, whether they're getting ten hours of sleep or twenty in each twenty-four hour cycle. Often it's not enough for the parents, whose own sleep is interrupted and whose day-time hours are taken up by this new and need-filled family member, but that's quite a different problem than the baby's needs not being met.

### Baby's Bedtime

There is no one "right" hour to put a baby to bed. Typical bedtimes range from 5:30 P.M. to 8:00 P.M., and by the same token, your baby's wake-up time might be as early as 5:00 A.M. or as late as 8:00 A.M. This will depend in part on his own internal circadian rhythms, in part on the way you've programmed him to conform to your family's habits, and in part on his sleep needs.

What is important is that you get him on some kind of schedule as early as you can and remain as consistent to that schedule as is practical. While rigidity is no virtue, you should maintain a reasonably consistent sleep schedule and put your baby to sleep at the same time every night, or close to it. If he is already eating strained foods or cereal, feed him about one hour before his bedtime at the same time every evening. (See Chapter 2 for an in-depth discussion of feeding.)

Of course, if your baby is clearly tired before his usual bedtime, you can put him to bed earlier than usual. Don't worry that he'll wake up too early as a result. If the baby is that tired, chances are he'll sleep longer than usual and wake up right around his usual time. But if not and he does wake up early the next morning, just put him down for his nap a little earlier than usual that day. He may nap a little longer than usual. Then, that night, you can settle him into bed at his usual time.

## Sleeping Through the Night

How soon should you expect your baby to "sleep through the night"? (Sleeping through the night is a misnomer, since we all—babies included—wake up at least briefly during the night.) Some babies give up their middle-of-the-night feedings as early as when they are eight weeks old. Almost all babies are able to sleep through the night by six months old.

Occasionally, a baby who has learned to sleep through the night will begin waking up again during the nighttime for no apparent reason. If your baby has given up night feedings and suddenly starts awakening during the night again and this happens more than just once or twice, try putting her to bed half an hour earlier. Though it seems odd, many parents find that this actually does solve the problem.

### Nature Takes a Hand

Sleeping at night is not just a habit learned in a world in which most activity goes on by day. It is also our biological destiny. Just as some species are naturally creatures of the night—such as bats, owls, and other nocturnal creatures—humans are by nature creatures of the day. Babies have this predisposition built into them.

Melatonin is a hormone produced in the pineal gland that is instrumental in helping people to get to sleep. It is secreted in greater quantities at night than by day. Apparently the darkness of night is a triggering factor, since the presence of artificial light has been demonstrated to affect melatonin production.

Babies, though, do not produce very much melatonin during the first few months of their lives. The little bit that is produced is produced at a consistent level—no higher by night than by day. Around the age of six months, however, a clear pattern in melatonin secretions emerges. The baby's system produces noticeably more of this hormone by night than by day. This coincides with the age at which babies begin to consolidate their sleeping hours, sleeping for a longer stretch at night and taking on average two distinct naps during the daytime hours.

## Ⓔ Essential

As your baby grows older and larger, his stomach will also grow in size and he will take in a greater quantity with each feeding. This will enable him to go for longer periods between feedings, which in turn will help him to sleep longer at a stretch.

The worst thing you can do is play the numbers game with your baby, but the average six-month-old spends approximately fourteen to fifteen hours a day sleeping, with a stretch of, on average, five hours of uninterrupted sleep at night.

### Learned Behavior

But it's not just melatonin production that influences the hours during which we sleep. Part of it is a learned behavior. Although humankind's biological disposition causes people to tend to sleep by night and be active by day, socialization takes over after that and plays a part as well. By wanting to fit in with the rest of the world, to be available to friends when they're available, to be available for work during the hours when most work is performed, to shop in stores when they're generally open, and to participate in most other activities, people learn that it's usually desirable to sleep by night and be awake by day. In order to keep pace with most of the rest of the world, human adults (and older children) reinforce the pattern that nature already suggests through melatonin production.

 *Alert!*

Your behavior with your baby when he wakes at night communicates that you expect him to sleep when it's dark. Resist the temptation to play with him when he awakens at night, even if you're still awake, or to show him off to guests who may be there if he awakens during the evening when you have company.

Babies, too, learn to sleep when the rest of the world is quiet and to be awake when those around them are. When your baby wakes up during the daylight hours and wants to be fed or held or played with, you usually respond positively. You feed her, generally without rushing. You take your time and talk to her and perhaps sing to her. You play with her and stroke her. But when she wakes up at night, you don't encourage wakefulness. You feed her or do whatever's needed, but you do it in more haste. You want her to go back to sleep, not only because she's supposed to be sleeping now, but because you're eager to return to your own sleep as well. Your behavior and your attitude send a subtle but recognizable signal to her.

Babies soon understand the message: Daylight hours are a time to play and be awake and to be active and involved. When it's dark, it's a quiet time when interaction is kept to a minimum and sleeping is encouraged.

## A Noise in the Night

Sleeping babies often make noises. If you hear sounds from your baby in her crib when she's been sleeping and before you assume she is hungry and crying, first be sure she is awake. Misguidedly, some parents will wake a baby for a feeding who is whimpering or making other noises in her sleep, or alternatively, they may offer her a bottle while she is still asleep. The baby may suckle in a half-asleep state and then return to sleep. But the fact is that the baby was not awake, was not crying, was not hungry, and did not need to be fed.

Whether out of concern for the baby's well-being or for the sake of their own peace and quiet, many parents are often too quick to feed a baby who isn't hungry. Not every cry signals hunger, and not every sound from a baby is a cry (or a demand for something). Babies do make sounds in their sleep, and these sounds should not concern you, nor do they signal any sort of need. These sounds are akin to an adult's talking in his sleep, nothing more, and they do not indicate a problem. Since babies do not yet talk, of course, the sounds they make in their sleep are not words but coos and even whimpers, but these sounds are not an indication that anything's wrong.

## *You Can't Fool Mother Nature*

The sleep patterns of newborns range wildly. Some babies in the months immediately following birth sleep for twenty hours out of the twenty-four that comprise a day; others sleep for as little as eight. Some babies sleep for only an hour at a time, while others sleep for stretches lasting as long as five hours. This seems to be the "luck of the draw," a difference inherent in each individual child and not something that the parents can change by darkening the baby's bedroom, keeping the ambient noise level down, or altering other external factors.

You may be able to influence the times at which your baby sleeps, but you cannot alter her sleep needs. If she needs only eleven hours of sleep out of each twenty-four, you may be able to influence which eleven hours out of the daily cycle she spends sleeping, but you will not have much luck in trying to get her to sleep more than eleven hours.

Because sleep is a biological function, going to sleep is as much a response to internal cues as to external ones.

Think about yourself and your own pattern of falling asleep: Do you go to sleep when you're tired or when you know you "should" go to sleep? If you go to bed before you're sleepy, you'll have trouble falling asleep, and you probably won't sleep soundly when you do fall asleep. If you try to stay awake beyond when you're sleepy and "ready for bed," you may find yourself in that state commonly known as overtiredness. When you're overtired, it's hard to fall asleep even though your body may have been clamoring for sleep for an hour or more.

 **Fact**

Firstborns tend to sleep less than babies who have at least one sister or brother. There are factors that can influence the child's sleep patterns after birth, though. Studies point to a connection between anxious parents, depressed parents, and parents who take a more active role in getting their child to sleep and children with problematic sleep patterns.

Babies, too, get tired and reach a point when they're "ready" for sleep. It's much easier to get your baby to sleep when he's ready than to put him in for the night or for a nap when you want him to sleep but he's wide awake. Nonetheless, establishing a good pattern of sleeping and wakefulness is desirable.

The answer? When it's possible, try to establish a sleep pattern for your baby that's consistent with his natural sleep pattern. If he's a child who naturally is ready to go to sleep at 6:00 P.M., don't plan his feeding time for 6:00 P.M. and bedtime for 7:00 P.M. By the same token, if he's a child who's ready for bed at 7:00 P.M., don't try to put him to bed at 6:00 P.M.

### Ⓔ Alert!

As long as your baby is getting enough sleep, it's unimportant for his well-being whether he goes to bed earlier and gets up earlier or goes to bed later and gets up later. His routine should be a combination of what best fits his natural biological clock and what doesn't disrupt the rest of the household.

Everyone—adult or child—has his or her own natural sleep pattern. Some of us are "larks," or early risers, and some of us are "night owls," who by nature stay up later and get up later. This is observable even in babies. Your baby may be inherently a lark or a night owl and may wake up happy and content or be cranky and slow to become fully alert when she wakes up.

## Chapter 2

# What's Keeping Baby Awake? Hunger, Schedules, and Pain

Adults often say that they "slept like a baby." But do babies really sleep that wonderfully? Any parent of an infant can tell you it's not so! Rare indeed is the baby who, at least in her early months, gets through the night without crying. She may cry because she wants food, because she's experiencing some discomfort, or simply because she's awake and would rather not be, but she doesn't know how to get herself back to sleep.

## *The Number One Internal Problem—Hunger*

If your baby is past the age at which she wakes up for night feedings, she might be unexpectedly hungry. If she no longer wakes up hungry at night, you may not think at first of feeding her when she wakes up, yet she might be hungry. She may simply not have eaten enough food or had enough milk at her last feeding. She may be growing enough so that she now needs more food or milk than what she's used to getting. It could just be a night on which she's particularly hungry.

Since the number one reason babies wake up at night is presumably hunger, it would make sense that you'd want to do anything you could to keep your baby from getting hungry during the night or at least from getting hungry as often. Wouldn't it be good if he weren't hungry and he didn't wake up to nurse or take a bottle? Even if you can't totally prevent his waking to feed during the night, anything you can do to minimize the number of times he does get hungry at night would be helpful. Let's look at the options.

### Breast versus Bottle

Are you breastfeeding your baby or feeding him an iron-fortified infant formula? If you're breastfeeding him, you may find that he wakes up more frequently during the night (as well as wanting to nurse more often during the day) as compared with the child of your friend who is formula-feeding. Breastfed babies tend to get hungry more often than formula-fed babies because breast milk, being such a natural product for your baby, is more easily ordered world and think that things run smoothest hey're determined by fixed schedules are drawn to g a baby according to a schedule. People who are reewheeling and relaxed are more likely to feed a ccording to the baby's apparent needs.

## n-Demand Feeding

o you always get hungry at exactly the same hour lay? No, you sometimes want lunch or dinner before e you usually eat, and at other times, you just aren't ngry even though it is your usual lunchtime or even dinner is on the table. Of course, you may have large or small breakfast or a late or early lunch, is what's affecting you, but other times there's no nt reason.

## act

your baby grows and her stomach grows, she'll take in re food at a time and need to feed less often. But if you d her on a schedule rather than on demand, you may realize that her needs have changed and she doesn't d feedings so close together anymore. One big advan- e to on-demand feeding is that you'll be more readily rt to your baby's changing needs as she grows.

ough your baby's food intake is much more regu- to amount (at least until he starts eating cereals and d foods), your baby's stomach also might feel empty

digested and passes out of his stomach more quickly than formula. But you shouldn't let that discourage you from nursing. Breast milk is very healthy, very natural, and very good for your baby.

The advantages of breastfeeding are many, including:

- Breastfeeding conveys a certain amount of immunity to the baby.
- Breastfeeding brings the child closer to his mom emotionally.
- Breastfeeding brings the mom closer to her child emotionally.
- Babies are very unlikely to have an intolerance to breast milk.
- Breast milk is easier to digest than formula.

There may be times when you'll want to give him a bottle instead of breastfeeding him. For instance, if Mom and Dad take turns getting up for the baby at night and it's Dad's turn or a babysitter is watching the baby, obviously nursing the baby is out of the question.

There is, of course, a way to give your baby breast milk even when it's Dad's (or Grandma's or the babysit-ter's) turn to feed: If Mom manually expresses some breast milk into a bottle at some point before bedtime or going out for the evening or uses a breast pump and then leaves the bottle of breast milk in the fridge, the baby can be fed breast milk from a bottle. Leaving some breast milk in a bottle will obviate the need to feed him formula.

### Solid Foods

One popular belief is that a baby who has eaten some solid food, rather than just drinking milk, will have a fuller stomach and will sleep longer. Is this true or false? Should you feed your baby a strained food or, for very young babies (around three months), some rice cereal for dinner just before bedtime with the hope that he'll sleep longer as a result?

The answer to that question depends on whom you ask. Doctors and other experts are divided in their opinions, and while some say it works, some say it doesn't. The American Academy of Pediatrics (AAP) is strongly positioned against giving cereal before an infant reaches the age of four to six months old.

### 🅔 *Alert!*

The younger a baby is when he starts solid foods, the more likely it is that he might develop food allergies. So wisdom suggests you not start too early. If you're in doubt, check with your pediatrician before introducing cereal or strained food into your baby's diet for the first time, whether you're doing it in an effort to help him sleep longer or just for general nutrition purposes.

The age at which your baby can go for longer stretches without feeding often coincides with the age at which solid foods such as rice cereal are introduced to his diet. Some experts who don't believe that solid foods help a

baby sleep longer believe that coincide theory they debunk. Because a baby re being able to eat rice cereal at about the grows, the two events coincide and app But actually, the baby would go for a lor awakening whether he's fed rice cereal Nature alone takes care of the problem to sleep for longer periods, regardless of solid food or simply given milk.

Solid food (which, for your baby, strained foods, as opposed to breast mil formula) is more easily digested when th than when the body is asleep. This is tru it's true for babies, too. For this reason, a to eat food other than milk should not be after dinner. You can still give your baby sleep, but give it at least an hour after he h or pureed carrots. Not only will allowing a dinner and bedtime give him a chance to more easily and completely, but it also w chance of his having tummy troubles the

### On-Demand Feeding versus Scheduled Feeding

Over the generations, "on-demand feedi uled feeding" have vied with each other method of offering a baby her nourishmen are no absolutes as to who is more likely on demand and who feeds by schedule,

a wel
when
feedi
more
baby

every
the ti
that
thou
had
whic
appa

late
stra

a bit earlier one day and somewhat later the next day. Does it make sense to feed him because "it's time," if he's not hungry? Does it make sense to make him wait when he's crying for a bottle or your breast because "it's not time yet"? Many parents (and many doctors) think it doesn't.

The obvious advantage to on-demand feeding is that you feed your child when she's actually hungry, not at an arbitrary hour determined by you. The disadvantage is that you may misread her cries and feed her when she really isn't hungry. If your baby is gaining too much weight, discuss your feeding routine with your pediatrician. If her weight is fine, on-demand feeding is probably working for you just fine.

### Scheduled Feeding

The obvious advantages to scheduled feeding are that you regulate the amount of food your baby gets by giving him feedings at certain hours only and that you can plan in advance for feeding him. You won't be in the middle of cooking dinner when suddenly you need to feed a crying, hungry baby. The disadvantage is that if your baby is hungry one-half hour or an hour before his scheduled feeding time, then you're going to have an unhappy baby on your hands from when he gets hungry until you finally feed him . . . and he's going to let you know about it.

If your baby's regular feeding time is 6:00 P.M. and she doesn't seem hungry, it's good to offer her a feeding anyhow in the interest of getting her to bed on schedule, whether that means a bottle, your breast, or solid foods, if she's eating them. Offer them to her, and she'll almost certainly eat. But if she cries at other times and especially if she seems to be hungry (for example, if she's sucking on her fist and is not a baby who does this habitually), then by all means offer her a bottle or your breast, even if it's not a regularly scheduled feeding time. If the baby is hungry, it's not good to be a slave to a schedule.

## Ⓔ *Question?*

**If I feed my baby on a schedule, does that preclude feeding her at night when she cries, if it's at a time when she's not scheduled for a feeding?**
While it's good to get your baby onto some sort of regular schedule (even babies who feed on demand self-regulate to some sort of loose schedule), it's not good to be rigid about it. Attempt to keep to a schedule but be flexible about it. You do nobody any good by strict adherence to feeding at arbitrary hours.

## *A Happy Trade-Off*

Here's an idea for the parents of babies who have given up waking for a 10:00 P.M. feeding but still get up to feed in the middle of the night: If your baby no longer wakes around 10:00 P.M. and now sleeps through until around 2:00 A.M. or so, try waking her for a feeding just before you go to bed. You may be able to forestall the middle-of-the-night feeding.

This is not a totally risk-free proposition. The main hazard here is that she might not get back to sleep easily, and you'll be left with a wide-awake (and possibly fussy) baby on your hands. The other disadvantage is that she will at some point no longer need that 10:00 P.M. feeding. Yet, if you continue to awaken her for it, you won't realize that she's reached a point at which it's unnecessary.

If she goes right back to sleep after the bottle or breast-feeding and if she doesn't wake up until at least 5:00 A.M. for another feeding, you can claim a victory in your quest for a better night's sleep for yourselves. You might want to consider trying this plan for a while.

What if you're feeding her on demand rather than on a schedule? Waking your baby for a 10:00 P.M. feeding as a means of precluding her waking up at 2:00 A.M. is feeding her on a schedule, rather than waiting until she demands food. The answer is that you can be a little bit flexible. You can feed your baby on demand the rest of the time and still wake her up at 10:00 P.M. for a feeding with a clear conscience. Rigidity has never been a virtue, and there's certainly no harm in feeding her on a combination of on-demand and scheduled feedings. So go ahead—give yourselves a break!

## When Your Baby's Schedule Doesn't Mesh with Yours

Your baby's natural sleep pattern may be so different from the rest of the family's routine that it's disrupting your household. If your baby is ready for sleep at 5:30 P.M. every evening and wakes up at 5:30 A.M. every morning, she is probably getting a good night's sleep, but it wreaks havoc on the rest of the family. Perhaps she shares a room with her older sister, who goes to bed at 7:30 P.M. and needs to keep the lights low and the noise down for two hours, from the baby's bedtime until her own. Perhaps you simply don't want to get up at 5:30 A.M. every morning, the hour at which your baby now wakes up. Maybe your baby is falling asleep at an hour that's too late for your family's schedule and is waking up too late for you to change her, feed her, dress her, and get her into the car in time to take her older sister to school.

## Ⓔ *Fact*

This ten-minute method also works if you need to adjust your baby's schedule to yours in spring for Daylight Savings Time and again in fall for Standard Time. It will help you gradually shift your baby's schedule to the "new time" in spring and again in fall, in just under one week.

### Resetting the Biological Clock

One option is to try to readjust your baby's schedule. Do it in ten-minute increments. Rather than trying to put her to bed an hour later or earlier, put her to bed ten minutes earlier or later, feed her ten minutes earlier or later, and move her schedule up or back by another ten minutes the next day. If you want to change her bedtime from 6:00 to 7:00 P.M., put her to bed at 6:10 P.M. on Monday, 6:20 P.M. on

Tuesday, 6:30 P.M. on Wednesday, and so on, and change the times of all her meals accordingly as well. There is a very good chance that you can reset her biological clock this way and bring her schedule around to one that better conforms to the rest of the family's schedule.

### Longer Days

If your baby has learned to distinguish light from dark, is aware of daylight, and thinks it's not time to go to sleep until it's dark out, you will need to darken his room so that you can get him to sleep at a reasonable hour in summertime. Otherwise he will be awake until later than you probably want him awake, and he will be up at the crack of daybreak. You may need "blackout shades," heavy curtains, drapes, or blinds. They're a worthwhile investment if your baby doesn't like to sleep during the daytime.

## Colic: Frequent Scapegoat, Real Pain

What is colic? What causes colic? No one, doctor or otherwise, is certain. Some experts feel it's a gastrointestinal disturbance in which a baby becomes particularly gassy. The name even hints at an intestinal connection—the word "colic" derives from the Greek "kolikos," the adjective form of "kolon," the large intestine. Others believe colic is simply a way for babies to blow off steam.

Depending on the baby, colic may peak at six weeks to three months. Most experts agree that colic disappears from the age of three months to one year, whether or not you take steps to quell it. Most everyone agrees that colicky babies cry severely, draw up their knees against their stomachs, and struggle when held. The crying spells tend to begin in the late afternoon or early evening, and the crying is intense and difficult to calm.

### Possible Help for Colic

Though sometimes it seems that nothing at all will help a colicky baby, suggested remedies include rubbing the baby's back while he's lying flat, offering him special diets and/or medicines that will calm him (consult your pediatrician), and simply holding him until the episode passes.

Some relief has been reported in some cases when the baby passes gas or has a bowel movement, which gives credence to the theory that colic is an intestinal upset. Yet, despite this evidence, not everyone agrees on the cause.

### Differing Points of View

Some doctors believe colicky babies are emotionally upset and have a need to cry, and if neither holding your baby nor offering him a pacifier helps, it may be a help to the baby to let him cry it out. In fact, some doctors prescribe sedatives for colicky babies, though not all doctors who do so subscribe to the emotional-cause theory; some who prescribe sedatives are simply trying to help the child settle down and are treating the effect, not the cause.

Some ten to twenty-five percent of newborns become colicky. There is no way of predicting which babies will be affected by colic.

Colic does not disappear overnight, but the hardest part of colic may be that the formerly colicky baby, now recovered, has become so used to being picked up, held, and comforted that he persists in wanting this treatment even after his colic has evanesced.

 **Fact**

Colic is not hereditary and does not necessarily run in the family. If your first baby is colicky, that does not indicate any particular likelihood that your next child and any other future children of yours will have colic.

## Teething

Of course, if he's not a newborn, his middle-of-the-night distress might be caused by teething. The eruption of teeth through sore and tender gums is a common cause of babies crying at night. (Teething probably also gets erroneously blamed more often than any other cause.) When a baby six months old or older suddenly becomes fussy at night, it's common for parents to assume "he must be teething." If your baby is drooling more than usual, seems to be biting things a lot, or if you can actually see or feel a tooth or a part of a tooth breaking through the gums, assume he really is teething. If he is, give him lots of soft things to chew on or offer him a teething toy, many of which are designed to be placed in the fridge or freezer between uses, since the coldness helps numb the baby's sore gums.

## *Intestinal Distress*

Intestinal pain could be the cause of your baby's unwillingness to sleep. If your baby is crying and having trouble sleeping, it could be a tummy ache that is causing her problems.

### Gas

If the baby is not crying because she is hungry, particularly if you just fed her, she may have a gas bubble and need to be burped. Babies, like anyone else, can also get plain old tummy aches. A tummy ache may result from a simple gas bubble (the most common cause) or something more complex. If your baby is one who needs burping, maybe you didn't get all the gas out when you burped her after dinner. If your baby is one who normally doesn't need burping, maybe just this once she has a stubborn gas bubble that she needs a little help dislodging. To try to dispel a gas bubble, hold her upright and rub her back in a circular motion.

### Ⓔ *Alert!*

Some babies burp naturally. Such a baby usually doesn't need to be burped by your rubbing or gently patting his back. But occasionally one of these babies gets a gas bubble in his tummy that he cannot dislodge on his own. Even if your baby is a "self-burper," it can't hurt to try to burp him in case that's the cause of his crying.

## Lactose Intolerance

Another cause of intestinal problems is lactose intolerance. This is an inability in the baby's system to digest lactose, or milk sugar. The baby who is lactose intolerant typically is fussy all the time, not only at night. (A less common possibility, but one you might also consider, is cow's milk protein allergy, in which case the culprit is not milk sugar but milk protein.) You should be particularly alert to the possibility of lactose intolerance if your baby suffers from frequent loose and/or foul-smelling bowel movements. If you suspect that your baby has lactose intolerance or cow's milk protein allergy, talk to your pediatrician. Switching your child to a soy-based formula or an elemental formula may alleviate the problem if an intolerance to cow's milk or to breast milk is the cause. If you are breast-feeding, first try eliminating dairy products from your own diet for a week or two and see if that doesn't make a big difference. Once there are no milk proteins to pass from your system into your breast milk as the result of your diet, your child's problem may well be alleviated.

If you've begun feeding your baby strained foods, she might also have an allergy to one of the foods you're feeding her. Even if she's not actually allergic, her stomach might simply be having a bit of trouble handling some food you've introduced. She might also be eating too much. An overfull tummy could make her feel uncomfortable and/or gassy.

**Chapter 3**

# Other Things Keeping Baby Awake

Naturally, many times when a baby wakes up and cries, she does so because she is hungry. However, many times, it is not hunger that wakes your baby. Some of the problems that may awaken your baby or keep her awake are serious ones. Others are less serious or not serious at all except that they disturb her sleep and possibly, as a result, yours. Teething, ear infections, and simple colds are among the conditions that commonly cause sleep problems.

## *Food Isn't Always the Answer*

Parents who are feeding on demand are advised to use a little common sense. Don't assume every cry is a cry for food. People often eat because they are bored, unhappy, or frustrated, and they are seeking comfort or enjoyment from food. Adults do it. Kids do it, too. Stop and think about when you last fed your baby. Has enough time elapsed that he should be hungry? Is it close to what you'd expect his feeding time to be? Is he demonstrating other indications of hunger, such as putting his fist in his mouth? Does he continue to cry or fuss even after you pick him up and hold him? If the answer to at least some of these questions is yes, you probably are right in giving him a bottle or your breast. But if not, look for the cause elsewhere, and if you can't find it, you may just have to hold him, rock him, soothe him, and try to calm him that way. If he's just finished a bottle an hour ago, the cause of his crying isn't very likely to be hunger.

## Ⓔ *Alert!*

If your child rubs his ear, especially if he has a cold, you can suspect the possibility of an ear infection. See your pediatrician.

Not only do you not want to teach your child that eating is the solution for every problem (you just might be training a future junk food junkie), but also feeding him won't even help in certain cases. If what caused him to cry wasn't hunger but boredom, feeding might make him sleepy and resolve the problem. But if it doesn't, he'll be just as bored when he finishes feeding, and he'll start crying again. The same is true if the cause of his unhappiness is a gas bubble. Feeding him might help push the gas through his system. But if it doesn't, he's going to be just as uncomfortable when he finishes feeding, and he'll start crying again. Now he has learned that feeding helps for a short time if he's uncomfortable or bored, even though it doesn't resolve the problem. He is laying the foundation for a lifetime of eating for all the wrong reasons, and you still have an unhappy baby on your hands once he's finished with the bottle or the breast.

So if you do feed your baby on demand and not by schedule, don't offer a bottle or your breast at the first cry unless it's been that long since his last feeding that he's logically due to be hungry again.

## *Anxieties*

The problem may even be an internal problem with an external cause: Your baby may be feeling anxious because he is picking up on your own anxieties. Though it is more often the parents of firstborns who are nervous and anxious, parents of children in any birth order can be especially anxious. This is particularly true if some outside situation is causing unusual anxiety in the parent. For example, if Mom is upset over a recent divorce, Dad has recently lost his job, Mom has quit her job to take care of the baby and is anxious about that situation, or if the grandparents have come for a long-term visit to help with the baby and Mom (or Dad) is anxious, Baby is going to sense it.

## Wide Awake in the Evening

Sometimes a baby will "go to sleep nicely" in the evening but wake up a couple of hours later and simply not be interested in going back to sleep. If it doesn't seem that he is hot or cold or otherwise troubled, you need to look for a reason elsewhere. There can be many reasons for this type of sleep disruption. Some of them are:

- This is a newborn who doesn't yet discriminate between day and night.
- This is an older baby, and he is more aware of what's going on in the household and, having woken up, wants to be part of the family's activity.
- Your baby is more sensitive to noises now that he's a little older, and the normal noise level in the house is now sufficient to wake him up.
- Your baby does not need as much sleep as he did previously, and so he has "taken a nap" rather than going to sleep for the night. Try putting him to bed later.
- Your baby did not drink enough breast milk or iron-fortified infant formula.

When this wasn't a problem before, why do babies suddenly start waking up hungry? Of course, if you're nursing, it could be a disruption in your milk flow. But if it's not that or if he's drinking from the bottle, the cause must lie elsewhere . . . within the baby himself.

Among the reasons for a baby not drinking enough to fill himself up sufficiently, count simple distractions as a prime suspect. When your baby is a newborn, although he's aware of the world around him, he'll zero in on your breast or the bottle and largely ignore all else around him. But as he grows older, he grows more aware of what's going on around him and is more easily intrigued by sights, motions, and sounds.

Within just a couple of months he can be distracted by the motion of a shadow on the wall as a tree branch waves outside the window in the path of incoming light from the sun or a street lamp. He can be distracted by his older brother zooming past him at top speed as he races through the house. He can be distracted by a loud voice suddenly emanating from the television. The world is full of distractions that clamor for his attention, and any of these can take him away from the task he's supposed to be set on: feeding.

## *Bad Dreams and Nightmares*

Though parasomnias (night terrors) are more easily identifiable by their symptoms to the parents of babies too young to talk about what has frightened them, bad dreams and nightmares are harder to pinpoint. At what age are babies capable of having such bad experiences in their sleep? It's hard to say. We know that by the age of two, toddlers are capable of having scary dreams.

But how much earlier can these incidents occur? Though no one can answer that with certainty, if your baby wakes up crying for no apparent reason, if he seems frightened, and if he clings to you, there's a good chance he's had a bad dream or a nightmare.

## Ⓔ *Question?*

**What causes a bad dream or nightmare in a baby?**
It is difficult to know for certain. Parents should avoid exposing their babies to scary television shows or movies, scary music, or even mildly scary games in the period shortly before bedtime, as these could contribute to scary dreams.

Certain medications and some foods can increase metabolism, which in turn can bring about nightmares. If your child appears to be having nightmares and this occurs more often than once in a while, talk to your pediatrician and see if he or she feels that anything in your baby's diet might be inducing these incidents.

### Time for TLC

If your child seems to have had a nightmare, comfort her, hold her, and reassure her. For very young kids, reassuring them that it was "only a dream" is useless. Even if your child is a toddler old enough to have a very limited vocabulary, she cannot understand the concept. Rather, cuddle her, stroke her, and show her that there's nothing to be afraid of. Leave a night-light lit, turn on a lamp on a low setting, or leave a hallway light on that will illuminate the room partly. Don't make it so bright that she'll have trouble falling asleep or get confused as to whether it's night or day, but do let her see that there's nothing lurking in the darkness waiting to get her.

If your child has experienced a nightmare and doesn't want to go back to sleep, it's okay for you to stay with her in her room for a little while. Hold her, rock her, then put her down in her crib and keep talking (or singing) to her, keep your hand in contact with her body, and encourage her with your soothing voice to go to sleep. If she has a "lovey" (such as a teddy bear) or if she uses a pacifier, offer it to her.

### Parasomnias/Sleep Terrors/Night Terrors

Parasomnia is an umbrella term that encompasses a number of behaviors occurring when a baby or toddler partially wakes from sleep in a state of terror and/or confusion. Though frightening, these incidents are more common among babies and toddlers than you may realize and occur to most children at least once. Children old enough to walk may sleepwalk.

The difference between night terrors and nightmares is that nightmares are dreams, which occur during REM sleep (active sleep), whereas night terrors occur as a child is coming up from non-REM sleep (quiet sleep), when he is not dreaming. How can you tell if your child is having nightmares or night terrors? In children old enough to talk, it's easier to distinguish. If, on the morning after the event, the child has no memory of it, it was almost certainly a night terror; nightmares often are remembered. An even better barometer is that babies (or older children) experiencing a night terror frequently don't recognize their parents and are generally confused, which is not true of nightmares. Another means of determining, which will work even with babies, is that night terrors usually occur within an hour or two of falling asleep; nightmares occur in the latter part of the night.

These incidents seem to occur when the child has been in a deep and dreamless sleep and he only partially awakens from it. It is difficult to get him fully awake if you try, even though he may be sitting up in his crib and/or thrashing around. If you try to comfort him or hold him, he may flail against you or resist you. He may return to sleep quickly on his own, or he may remain semi-awake for as much as half an hour before returning to sleep, most commonly to a deep sleep.

### Ⓔ *Essential*

Many parents worry that their children who have parasomnias are exhibiting symptoms of a psychological problem or disturbance. This simply isn't so. Though the child appears to be terrified—and the parents, witnessing the event, most surely are terrified—parasomnias are not in any way indications of anxiety, depression, hallucinations, or any other psychological problem.

### Indications of Sleep Terror

Your first indication that your child is experiencing a sleep terror is likely to be a scream or shriek that sounds different from his usual cry. His facial expression may cause him to look horribly frightened. Other physical indications that may be present include dilated pupils and rapid breathing. In addition, your baby may appear sweaty, and if you put your hand on his chest, you may find his heart racing.

Certain factors can predispose a child to experience sleep terrors:

- **Sleep deprivation and, indirectly, stress.** Sleep terrors are more likely to occur the night after a bad or incomplete night's sleep. Though psychological problems do not cause parasomnias, stress can be an indirect cause in that stress causes sleep loss and sleep loss in turn can bring on night terrors.
- **Sleeping in a strange place.** Even a "happy" strange place—a hotel room or cottage on a vacation or a night spent at Grandma's—can predispose a child to an incident of parasomnia.
- **Illnesses, especially those accompanied by high fever.** Even a child who has never before experienced night terrors may have such an event under these circumstances.
- **Certain medications.** If your child has recently begun taking a new prescription and begins experiencing night terrors, check with your pediatrician to see if something more than mere coincidence is at work here.

- **Sleep apnea.** Because your baby who has sleep apnea is transitioning from deep sleep to wakefulness suddenly and more often, she is more subject to parasomnias than the average baby.

Parasomnias, though scary to the parents, are not dangerous to the baby. In older children who may sleepwalk, there is a danger of them falling down stairs or even out a window, even though sleepwalking children can see where they are going; but babies confined in cribs, even if they are old enough to walk, are fairly immune to such dangers.

## Ⓔ *Fact*

Parasomnias tend to run in families. If your first child experiences night terrors or any other form of parasomnias, there's a better-than-average chance that your next child(ren) will, too, and also a good chance that one or both parents experienced them, whether or not you or your spouse are aware that you did.

### Handling Parasomnia

If your baby experiences an occurrence of parasomnia, don't try to wake him during it. Though the old adage that waking him will harm him is simply not true, what it will do is make the event last longer. Don't try to comfort him, either, as it will only agitate him. In fact, there is not much you can or should do that is proactive during the course of the event, but you can try to settle the child back down and comfort him and then settle him back to sleep once the event is over. Your best proactive move is preventive: Try to ensure that he sleeps long enough and on a regular schedule so as to preclude avoidable recurrences. You may not be able to avoid all occurrences of parasomnia, but knowing that certain factors, including sleep deprivation, make an occurrence more likely means you're better able to prevent them.

## Myclonic Jerks

Another minor problem that may affect babies is "myclonic jerks." Even if you're not familiar with the term, you're undoubtedly familiar with the event. It's likely happened to you yourself. You're in bed, you're half asleep or more so, and suddenly your body or part of your body twitches or jumps in place as you lie there, and you wake up with a start. They happen to babies, too. But while you know what it is or at the very least know that it's nothing serious, a baby will be more easily startled by such an occurrence. If you experience a myclonic jerk and you have trouble falling right back to sleep, you may be momentarily upset at this intrusion into your near-sleep state, but you won't start crying. But you're not six weeks old or six months old or sixteen months old.

So if you put your baby to bed for the night, he seemed to be drifting off happily, and a short while later he's crying again, consider that the problem may well be that he has experienced a myclonic jerk and now is suddenly and unhappily awake again. It's nothing for you to be concerned about. If only you could explain it to him, you could let him know that it's nothing for him to be concerned about, either. But it will require him soothing himself back to sleep again, perhaps with a bit of help from you.

Besides "motor sleep starts," as myclonic jerks are sometimes called, there are also "visual sleep starts," in which the sleeper has the sensation of bright light suddenly flashing inside the eyes or inside the head, and "auditory sleep starts," consisting of a loud noise, something like a snap, which seems to emanate from inside the head.

## Ⓔ *Essential*

It can be frightening for a parent to view myclonic jerks in her baby, if she doesn't know what she is witnessing. Some parents mistake myclonic jerks for a form of seizure, but assuredly they are not. In all probability, it is not a seizure, a precursor of a seizure, or any kind of problem. It is very, very normal. However, as infantile spasms can look a lot like myclonic jerks, do be wary and take note of the event in case you see repeated occurrences.

### Sleep Apnea

You've probably heard the term "sleep apnea"; you may even have it yourself or know someone who does. In this condition, a sleeping person stops breathing while asleep. Within a brief period, his brain recognizes that breathing has ceased and wakes him up. At that point, now awake, he resumes breathing, but his sleep has been disturbed. The person with sleep apnea may wake many times during the night in order to resume breathing and, as a result, does not get a restful night's sleep.

Surprisingly enough, babies, too, can suffer from sleep apnea. The baby who wakes once, several times, or many times during the night due to this condition does not get a good night's sleep—and, typically, neither do his parents. Unless the baby is a good self-soother, he will want his parents' help in settling down again. Since sleep apnea sufferers often wake with a start, even good self-soothers may cry when they wake with an incidence of sleep apnea.

But what if your baby self-soothes and goes back to sleep on his own? What indications can you look for that might cause you to suspect your child may have sleep apnea?

- The baby may appear sleepy or be cranky due to sleepiness during the day because his nighttime sleep is being interrupted, or he may be hyperactive due to being overtired.
- He may snore at night. Not all babies who snore suffer from sleep apnea, but almost all babies (and adults) who suffer from sleep apnea snore.
- You may notice, as you observe him sleeping, that there are pauses in his breathing when he seems not to be breathing at all. (This may also simply be a case of periodic breathing, which is more common at this age and usually considered normal.)
- He may be breathing through his mouth.

- The baby may sweat profusely, a situation that in some cases seems related to sleep apnea.
- He may cough or choke often in his sleep.

## Ⓔ Fact

Though such factors as illness, extra body weight, and receding chins can all cause sleep apnea in children, the most common causes are adenotonsillar hypertrophy and the neuromuscular tone of the upper airway during sleep, and enlarged tonsils and/or enlarged adenoids, which can obstruct the airway and interfere with breathing. Children who have Down syndrome also are at greater risk, due to the prevalence of being overweight that accompanies this condition and because Down syndrome children often have enlarged tongues, which can obstruct the airway.

## Other Sleep-Disturbing Breathing Problems

A television show that showed home videos once aired a tape of a baby snoring loudly. Yes, it was funny, but it should also have signaled the parents to at least mention it to their pediatrician. Any unusual sound made by your baby is cause for further exploration.

### Snoring

Snoring, though it's a problem usually thought of as pertaining to adults, can also disturb a baby's sleep. Is your baby a noisy breather and/or a mouth breather? The sound of his own noisy breathing, even though short of actual snoring, can awaken a sleeping baby.

### Mouth-Breathing

Mouth-breathing can leave the mouth dry and uncomfortable, also waking your baby. He may cry because he feels thirsty or because his mouth is dry. Mouth-breathing almost always occurs when there is nasal congestion but can occur in some babies for other reasons. It is pretty easily observable by the parents. If you note that your baby is a mouth-breather, mention it to your pediatrician.

### 🄴 *Alert!*

All these issues are medical problems and need to be discussed with your baby's pediatrician. From sleep apnea to GERD, there are approaches to the problem, but first your pediatrician needs to be aware that your baby has this problem. So if you suspect one of these problems in your baby, discuss it promptly with your baby's doctor.

### Coughing and Choking

There's another breathing problem that can disturb your baby's sleep: Your baby may be coughing or even choking during the night. Choking can be caused by mucus dripping from the nose, by a burp that isn't pure gas but contains some partially digested foods, or by gastroesophageal reflux. GERD (Gastro-Esophageal Reflux Disease), another condition usually thought of in connection with adults, is found in a surprising number of children as well, including babies.

## Sleep Talking

Sleep talking is not a problem in any real sense of the word. Sleep talking may on occasion wake your baby when it occurs, but most of the time he'll sleep through it. It's more of a topic of confusion or concern for the parents than it is for the child.

Of course, when it occurs with a two-month-old or seven-month-old, sleep talking doesn't consist of words but rather of coos and other sounds. Clearly a child too young to talk is not going to suddenly spout words in her sleep. But she is "talking in her sleep" all the same.

Parents who hear coos or other vocalizations coming from the crib of their child who is supposed to be asleep may assume, most understandably, that the child has awakened for some unknown reason and is babbling in her crib. But if you go to your child's room at night, after she has gone to sleep, and see that she is lying there with her eyes closed although her mouth is moving, it is probably safe to assume that she is "talking" in her sleep.

You don't need to do anything about it unless she wakes herself up in the process. It is not an indication of a problem. It is not the sign of a psychological disturbance. It does not mean your baby is awake. Relax. She is simply talking in her sleep. If she wakes up, comfort her and return her to her crib—with her pacifier or "lovey" if need be. Otherwise do nothing. All is well.

## External Problems

There are some problems that are outside the realm of the physical body. They can be the easiest to solve because you usually have control over your home environment. Some external factors that might disrupt sleep are the "climate" and the level of noise and light in your baby's room. Diapers, clothing, and other minor annoyances may also present problems that can be quickly remedied.

### Temperature

Another culprit to be alert for is a room temperature too warm or too cold for your baby's comfort. Indications that your baby is too warm include:

- She is sweaty.
- She has damp hair.
- She has a heat rash.
- She is breathing rapidly.

## (E) Essential

Disposable diapers negate the need for diaper pins, but if your child is wearing cloth diapers and you have them fastened with diaper pins, by all means check to see if your baby has a very pointy, painful reason for crying.

## Humidity

Besides temperature, consider the humidity level. If it's too dry or too humid in the room, your baby may have trouble breathing comfortably. Does the temperature in the room seem comfortable to you? How does your baby's skin feel when you touch him? Does he feel sweaty or chilled? Adjust the room temperature or house temperature, adjust the clothing your baby is wearing, putting lighter or heavier pajamas on him, or add a light blanket or remove one.

If the room air is too dry or too humid, a humidifier or dehumidifier should solve the problem. Be aware, though, especially if your baby exhibits allergy symptoms, that using a humidifier can increase dust mites and mold and make allergies worse.

## Fear of the Dark

If you suspect the problem is fear of the dark, the answer is, obviously, turning on a night-light. Banishing scary shadows is nearly as easy. If simply turning on a night-light doesn't rid the room of the shadows you suspect may be bothering your baby, then look to eliminate them at the source. Close the blinds more tightly or draw the curtains if the shadow is of a tree branch or other object outside the house. If the shadow emanates from a hallway light fixture or other object inside the house, alter the lighting that's casting the shadow, close the baby's room door partway, or make other necessary changes.

## Diapers

Although newborns don't usually cry due to wet or dirty diapers, older babies do. Check his diaper to see if it needs changing. When your baby gets a little older, he'll want his diaper changed as soon as it needs it. Suddenly he begins crying "for no apparent reason." The reason will become all too apparent if you check his diaper; it's simply a situation that didn't register with him before this and didn't used to make him cry to get it fixed. Now that he's not as young as he used to be, he's become aware of it when his diaper needs changing.

Even in newborns, you shouldn't ignore a wet or messy diaper since it can lead to diaper rash, and that is a situation that will bother even the youngest of babies.

## One Thing Leads to Another

Diaper rash itches and burns and is no fun! If your baby is up in the middle of the night, fussing and crying, and doesn't seem to be hungry, or it isn't an hour when you'd expect him to be hungry, or he no longer wakes for feedings, he may be crying because he has a diaper rash. Check and see if he has a red rash or irritation under his diaper, and if he does, apply a soothing lotion or ointment that's especially formulated for diaper rash. (You can get such preparations over-the-counter at your drugstore.) Even more important, prevent diaper rash by changing his diaper as soon as it needs to be changed and by wiping his bottom (front and back) with a soft wipe product when you change him. It's better to eliminate the causes of diaper rash preventively than to treat the condition after the fact.

### Clothing

Maybe the problem is that your baby's clothing is too tight. Do his pajamas (or other sleep clothes) still fit him? Has he outgrown what he's wearing?

## Ⓔ *Alert!*

Sleep habits tend to continue; so if your baby wakes up crying, it's something to address for the long haul and not just for now. Once she becomes accustomed to crying out for you at night and having you come and comfort her, a pattern can easily establish itself, even when the cause of discomfort has been removed.

The cause of your baby's discomfort may be something minor yet annoying to the baby: It could be that he's gotten a hair wrapped around his finger, which is bothering him. It could be that one of his fingernails is long or ragged and is scratching his face, or one of his toenails is long or ragged and is scratching his other leg when he moves his feet. If you don't find an obvious cause for his discomfort and burping doesn't help, consider looking for a problem such as one of these.

## Chapter 4

# Signal When Ready

Sports teams use signals to let each other know what type of play will be attempted next. Signals are very useful, and you and your baby can make good use of them, too. You can send signals to your baby that will tell him when it's time to go to sleep and when it's time to be awake and playful. He can send signals to you, even though he doesn't know he's doing it, which will let you know when he's ready to go to sleep.

## Early Cycles

When you first bring your baby home from the hospital, you'll likely let her determine when she's going to go to sleep and when she's going to be awake for a while. Before her sleep consolidates, she'll wake from a sleep cycle, probably hungry, and nurse or have a bottle. She'll stay awake for two hours or possibly even longer and then go to sleep again on her own or perhaps with the aid of another bottle or nursing again. Then she'll sleep for a few hours before waking again. Once she begins to sleep for longer stretches at a time, her sleep cycles may become more manageable.

You can try putting her to bed at an earlier hour or a later hour to help modify her schedule so that it's more convenient for and compatible with your family's schedule. Sometimes you need to try to maneuver your baby into sleeping when you want her to, even before her sleep begins to consolidate. This is particularly true with the baby who wakes in the middle of the night and seems unable to go back to sleep.

## Do Routines Matter?

A child's or baby's bedtime routine actually begins before his bedtime itself. The run-up to bedtime is important, too. If you normally put your baby to sleep very shortly after dinner, try to stick to this same schedule every night, so that your baby learns to expect this. He knows that he'll be put into his crib within a brief time after his bottle, or after nursing, or in the case of an older baby, after being fed his dinner of baby food.

In the half hour or so just before bedtime, avoid activities that will overstimulate him and get him, worked up and active. Chances are you wouldn't play bouncing games or similar activities with him anyhow right after dinner. That's a definite invitation to a messy disaster! But there are other games that can overstimulate him too, such as tickling games or versions of peek-a-boo in which you crouch down beside the crib, beneath his level of vision, and then jump up and make a silly, scary noise to make him laugh. If he starts laughing very hard and getting very excited, it will get him worked up, make him more active, and make it harder for him to settle down and go to sleep. What not to do is as important as what you should do, and getting your baby all revved up is definitely a no-no.

## Ⓔ *Essential*

If you leave a grandparent, babysitter, or other person in charge of your baby and you expect this person to put your baby to bed, explain your usual bedtime ritual to them so that they can follow it as closely as possible. This will help in getting your baby to go to sleep successfully.

## Signs That Baby Is Ready for Bed

You've been holding him or rocking him and snuggling him, but he's still awake. The last two times you tried putting him back in his crib, he started screaming again. How will you know when he's finally getting sleepy and might be ready to try to get to sleep again?

### A "Sleepy" Checklist

There are subtle and some not-so-subtle signs your baby will give when he's ready to go to sleep. These same signs are good indications at any hour, not just the middle of the night. What are they?

- He gets a bit fussy even though you're holding him.
- He yawns.
- He pulls at his ear.
- He rubs at his eyes.
- He sucks on his fingers. (This last one is a less accurate signal. It may indicate sleepiness, hunger, or neither of these things.)

## ⓔ *Alert!*

If you see your baby displaying one of these "sleepy" signals, don't ignore it. Some parents make the mistake of thinking, "Let me make sure he's good and sleepy before I put him back in his crib, so he'll be sure to go to sleep easily." This is a fallacy in logic. A baby who is overtired has even more trouble getting to sleep.

Do you observe him giving you one of those signals? Then now is the time to try again to get him to go to sleep.

## *Establish Regular Sleep Habits and Routines*

Regular sleep habits are useful. It helps if he gets used to being put down for the night at around the same time every day. Before your baby reaches the age of six weeks or so, it's too early to try to help him learn this necessary skill, even though he may sometimes fall asleep on his own in the crib. Around the age of six weeks, he's old enough that you can start helping him learn to go to sleep without being rocked, put in a swing, or otherwise helped by you. Now he's ready for you to try to regulate the times he's awake and the times he sleeps, as well as his feeding times.

## Ⓔ *Essential*

Though some babies sleep happily in the dark without a night-light, especially those whose rooms receive some light even through closed blinds or curtains, most babies will be more comfortable if the room has a soft glow to it. Your baby may be made fearful by the darkness or by shadows that appear on his walls or ceiling. Perhaps a tree branch, backlit by a streetlight, shows up as a menacingly moving figure on his wall due to an improperly closing shade, or maybe a hall light outside the open door of his room casts the shadow of his door or of something in the hallway. A night-light can dispel the darkness, the shadows, and the fears that go with them.

### More Elements of a Bedtime Routine

You can make the bedtime routine as simple or as elaborate as you want. Older kids brush their teeth before they go to bed; babies, still toothless at six weeks, obviously are too young for brushing teeth. But there are other things you can do with babies to signal to them that settle-down time is approaching.

How does your baby feel about baths? While many babies go through a brief period of being afraid of bathing, most babies enjoy it most of the time. If your baby enjoys the warm, soothing water, his bath can be part of his prebed routine. Not only is the water soothing to your baby, but your touch as you wash him gently also soothes him. If your baby is a child who finds his bath a relaxing experience, there's a natural way to get him calm and ready to drift off to sleep when he gets into his crib.

After he's had his bath and you've toweled him off, get him into his pajamas or whatever clothing he customarily wears to bed. Now is a good time to close the blinds and/ or curtains and to turn off all the lights except his nightlight. You can carry him as you perform these tasks. He'll soon learn to associate all these activities with the fact that it's time to go to bed and go to sleep.

### Beyond the Bath

After the bath, what's next? Perhaps a lullaby. A lullaby doesn't have to be a traditional song about going to sleep, such as *Rock-a-Bye Baby*. (For a lullaby that isn't about the cradle and the baby falling from the treetop, try *Hush, Little Baby* [Mama's gonna buy you a mockingbird] instead.) Any soft song will do. It might be an old childhood favorite, a nursery rhyme for which you know a tune it's been set to, or a popular song with a gentle rhythm and a slow tempo.

Too many parents are inhibited about singing to their babies because, at best, they have poor singing voices and, at worst, they can't carry a tune. But the reality is that your baby is no music critic. She cares only that her mom or dad is singing to her and holding her or singing to her and touching her as she lies there in her crib. She's not listening to you critically.

## Ⓔ *Fact*

At age six weeks or six months or eighteen months, your baby is no judge of singing ability. All she hears is the love in your voice, and that's all you should be concerned about, too. Squeaky voice? Rusty voice? Off-tune or off-key? It doesn't matter. All she needs to hear is a soothing tune, sung with love.

Besides singing a lullaby or some other soothing song that can serve as a lullaby, you can talk to your child or tell her a story. Though some parents think that telling fairy tales to a child six months old (or a child of any age too young to understand what you're saying) seems silly, many others understand that it's actually very wise and helpful.

### The Soothing, Familiar Voice

Your child learns to recognize your voice at an early age. Even though she doesn't understand the words or the concepts of angry, teasing, happy, or soothing, she can differentiate at an early age between a scolding tone and a loving one. She will be upset by the former and soothed by the latter. You can use your voice—your speaking voice, not just your singing voice—to comfort and soothe your child, not only at any time when she's upset and crying, but also at bedtime when you want to settle her down.

One way to do this is certainly to tell her a bedtime story, whether you read fairy tales or other suitable fare from a book, tell her a story from memory, or even make one up. Another thing you can do is tell her a make-believe story about herself: "Once upon a time, there was a baby named Jill who lived on a fluffy pink cloud" or tell her a true story about herself—perhaps about something that happened that day.

One more thing you can say and do that may be meaningful to both of you is to offer up a bedtime meditation or prayer. Just as is true of *Rock-a-Bye Baby,* the most famous old standard lullaby, whose words are scary, you may not wish to offer up the most famous old standard bedtime prayer, either. In case you forget, the words to "Now I Lay Me Down to Sleep" include "If I should die before I wake." While your baby won't understand these words at this age, any more than he can understand the lines in the lullaby about the baby falling, if you get in the habit of offering this prayer and continue to use it, there will come a day when your child will understand the words. As an alternative to saying a prayer, you can read poetry, song lyrics, or anything that has a cadence that can lull your baby to sleep.

## When to Break the Rules

You know that it's important to put your baby to sleep at a regular time, but you also know that it's important to put him to sleep when he shows signs of sleepiness. Suppose that because of an interrupted nap or for some other reason, your baby shows signs of sleepiness an hour before his usual bedtime. You may be wondering what you should do then: put him in an hour early or try to keep him awake for an hour longer?

You're better off putting him in an hour early, regardless of the fact that you're trying to get him on a schedule. If you keep him up, one or both of two things will happen: He'll get fussy and cranky because he's tired, and/or he'll get overtired and have trouble falling asleep when you do put him to bed. Better to forgo the schedule and put him in when he shows signs of needing to sleep.

## Ⓔ *Alert!*

If you do rock him, hold him, or cuddle him in your effort to soothe him to sleep, do it only to the point of his growing drowsy, not to the point of his falling asleep. You can also put him in his crib and keep your hand on him and sing to him or talk to him. But remove your hand, and remove yourself from his room, before he falls asleep.

## Don't Establish Bad Habits

You don't want your baby to learn to need to be rocked, cuddled, held, or even just to be in contact with your hand, or to need to hear your voice, or to be aware of your presence in order to fall asleep. The goal is to learn to help your baby to become able to go to sleep on his own without your help. This is, of course, helpful when you first put him in bed for the night, but it is a particularly important skill for him to learn in order that he can get himself back to sleep on his own when he awakens during the night. Naturally, if he awakens because he's too hot, he's hungry, a diaper rash is bothering him, or he has some other real need, he's still likely to cry for you. If he awakens in order to move around a bit in his crib or simply because he's moving from one phase of sleep to another, you want him to be able to settle back down to sleep again on his own.

## Settling Baby into His Crib

Generally, a good bedtime for babies is somewhere between 7:00 P.M. and 8:30 P.M., depending on your family's routine and on the baby's own internal clock. Is she naturally an early riser or a late riser, and does she show signs of sleepiness or tiredness earlier in the evening or later on? Whatever time you settle on as her bedtime, try to stick to it pretty consistently, though you don't have to be a slave to routine. If your family is out visiting friends or family and your late return delays your baby's bedtime a bit for one night, it's not the end of the world, even though it's certainly not desirable. Try to plan so that this sort of interruption to the routine doesn't happen, but if it does, don't be upset by it. You can get your baby's schedule back on track the next night.

## Nighttime Attire

It's really best if your baby wears something different to bed than she wears all day. This will help signal to her that it's time for something different—going to sleep. She will eventually learn to associate her pajamas (or whatever her night attire is) with bedtime. Besides, the pajamas or other bedtime attire that you'll put your baby to sleep in, you may want to swaddle her (wrap her tightly in a blanket or small sheet). (For a fuller description of swaddling, see Chapter 5.)

## Something to Look At

In addition, some babies enjoy having something to stare at as they drift off to sleep. Though winding up her crib mobile for her as a sleep-inducer isn't recommended, she can still stare at the mobile in its immobile state as she drifts off. What are some of the things your baby might enjoy looking at as she settles down to sleep?

- A crib mirror, in which she can peer at herself
- A crib toy she can gaze at
- A brightly colored, engaging picture hanging on the wall

## A Positive Attitude

Attitude is important in getting a child to sleep successfully—both your attitude and the baby's. If you tense up because you're dreading the possibility that he won't go right to sleep, he'll sense your tension and react to it. If you rush because you're in a hurry to get him to sleep so you can enjoy dinner with your spouse, or because another child is waiting for you to tuck him in, or because you're simply eager to relax alone, you won't communicate the peacefulness and ease that you want to convey to your baby.

His attitude is important, too. Though babies can't form the thought that older kids can, "if I go to sleep now I might miss out on something fun," they can and often do feel separated from their parents by being put to bed away from where their parents are and where things are happening. It's very helpful to make going to bed a very positive and enjoyable experience for your baby, one that he'll learn to look forward to.

## Ⓔ *Essential*

You should look forward to and enjoy the bedtime rituals you establish as much as your baby enjoys them. Don't perceive them as merely a means to an end. Yes, they will help you get your child to sleep more easily, but let the rituals of his bedtime become a pleasure unto themselves. You and your baby can actually both enjoy bedtime! It can also be a major bonding experience.

## *Recognizing Night and Day*

As you learned earlier, babies may have a predisposition to sleep when it's dark out and there's less activity going on inside the house, but their bodies don't produce much melatonin, the hormone that helps us to feel sleepiness, until they're six months old or so. Your baby may be one of those who spends many of the nighttime hours in sleep from the beginning. But if not, there are a number of things you can do to help the situation.

To begin with, you can darken his room at night and try to send him signals in this way that it's nighttime, not time for play or wakefulness. You can decline to play with him when the room is dark and it's night. If he cries, you can hold him and soothe him, but this isn't the time for a game of "This Little Piggy." It will take him a while to get the message, but stick with it. Don't ignore his cries, but show him that nighttime is not playtime.

Some parents of babies who don't know night from day make the mistake of trying to keep their babies awake by day in order to get them tired enough to sleep at night. This tactic frequently backfires: The baby becomes over-tired and has trouble falling asleep at night. This method is not recommended. You can let your baby sleep but try to keep him from sleeping for an extended stretch of four to five hours. This way, he is more likely to sleep better at night and not be so overtired that he can't fall asleep.

### Working by Day to Insure a Good Night

Here are some tips that may help keep your baby engaged and alert during the day so that he does more of his sleeping at night.

- Keep the lights bright in Baby's room or whatever room Baby is in during the day.

- Keep a stereo, radio, or other source of background noise going.
- Talk to Baby and interact with him physically (such as by playing games with him) as much as practical.
- If he takes an extended nap, consider waking him up after three hours or so.
- As much as possible, plan car trips (errands and such) either at times when you would expect Baby to be napping or just after a nap, when he is least likely to succumb to the lulling motion of the car. In other words, try not to let car trips provide an occasion for extra daytime naps.

### Ⓔ *Essential*

Making sure your baby gets plenty of light during the day, including sunlight at the window or around his shaded carriage when possible, will help her distinguish day from night. This is not to say that you should expose your baby to continued direct sunlight, which is not recommended.

### *When Baby Is Overtired*

Overtiredness has already been addressed in a few places in this book, but it bears revisiting here: The child who is overtired is a child who will have trouble falling asleep. You've probably seen this phenomenon in older kids, and it's more easily identifiable in kids old enough to run around the house: They get wired, and they run around crazily, seemingly wide-awake and full of energy. They're wild, they're loud, they're active, and they seem anything but sleepy. But the fact is, they're overtired. Overtiredness makes it difficult for a person of any age, adults included, to fall asleep.

That's why it's important to put your baby to bed when he seems sleepy, even if it's not yet his regular bedtime. That's also one of the reasons why it's important to honor his regular bedtime and not try to keep him awake for frivolous reasons (such as showing him off to company).

## Teaching Baby to Get Herself Back to Sleep

At first, your baby will wake up during the night for feedings. Later, she'll outgrow the middle-of-the-night feedings but may still wake up. We've already discussed some of the reasons. She may have a bona fide need, such as being too warm or being thirsty, or she may simply have woken up to move around or roll over. This is no problem unless she cannot get herself back to sleep again, known as "self-soothing."

If your baby does wake up during the night, what should you do? First of all, do nothing for a few minutes. Your baby may wake up, make a little bit of noise as she finds herself awake at an unwanted hour, and then slowly settle down and go back to sleep. If you hear your baby making cooing noises, soft cries, or anything other than a full-throated wail, don't go running into her room. Let her work her way back to sleep on her own. If she can't, she'll let you know . . . quickly!

If she doesn't settle down quickly, then by all means go to her. Though there is a school of thought that advocates letting your baby cry herself to sleep once you are sure that she is not hungry, hot or cold, in need of burping, or otherwise in discomfort, most experts disagree with this thinking. After all, something is bothering the baby, even if it is merely her inability to get back to sleep. She is seeking help of some sort, even if it is only the comfort of your presence and companionship at a time when she is awake and doesn't want to be. She cannot speak and cannot tell you what is troubling her. All she can do is cry. It is her only form of communication.

Ⓔ **Fact**

For years, parents have said of the child who cries little or who sleeps well through the night that "She's a good baby." But babies who sleep through the night or who cry relatively little are not being "good." This is not a question of behavior. The reverse of the coin would imply that a baby who cries a lot or doesn't sleep well is "bad." Assuredly such a baby is not misbehaving or deliberately being difficult. Instead of saying that your baby is "good" or "bad," say "She's an easy baby" or "She has her moments."

There was a time when it was believed that crying was "natural" for babies, that crying helped them expand their lungs, and that crying was "merely a baby's way of expressing herself," but that school of thinking has been replaced by the belief that babies cry only if something is bothering them. You should try to find out what the problem is and resolve it if possible. If a resolution is not possible, you should at least provide comfort.

### Is Baby the Right Age to Go to Sleep on His Own?

Until your baby is about six weeks old, his cycles of sleeping and waking are likely to be somewhat haphazard. He might sleep for two hours at a stretch, perhaps longer, and then wake up. This cycle of wakefulness could last from just long enough to have a bottle or nurse at your breast and then go to sleep again to a span of two or more hours, perhaps even long enough for him to want to feed again before he goes back to sleep. If you're lucky, he'll spend many of the nighttime hours asleep, but in these early weeks of his life, this is by no means guaranteed. At this age, it's too early to try to establish regular routines.

Ⓔ *Essential*

In trying to set bedtimes and naptimes for your baby, you'll want to take two things into account: her own internal schedule and your family's schedule. What time does she get sleepy on her own? What time does she wake up if left to wake up on her own? How does this mesh with your family's schedule?

If you're feeding him on schedule, rather than on demand, you may begin to set a routine for feedings, but until his sleep consolidates and he begins sleeping for longer stretches at a time, it's difficult or even pointless to try to get him to sleep at certain set hours.

At around six weeks, he'll begin to sleep more during the night (interrupted by periods of wakefulness when he'll feed and, hopefully, go back to sleep quickly). His daytime sleeping will decrease in quantity. Some time later (though not at the same exact age for every baby), his daytime sleeping will consist of a morning nap and an afternoon nap, and during the rest of the daytime he'll be awake and alert.

If your baby naturally seems tired and sleepy every night around 7:00 P.M., that time would probably be a good bedtime for him. Suppose, though, that Mom and Dad both work. Mom gets home at 5:30 P.M., and Dad doesn't get home until 7:15 P.M. Dad wants to see Baby while Baby is still awake, but with a 7:00 P.M. bedtime for Baby, that isn't working out to Dad's advantage. You could try repatterning your baby's sleep schedule so that he goes to bed at 7:30 P.M. or 8:00 P.M. instead. On the other hand, maybe your usual family dinnertime is 7:00 P.M., and you'd like your baby to go to sleep at 6:00 P.M. so that you can spend an hour in the kitchen, preparing the meal. In that case, you might want to try to adjust your baby's schedule so that he goes to bed at 6:00 P.M. As explained earlier, the best way to adjust a baby's sleep schedule is in increments of ten minutes at a time until you have moved his bedtime up or back to the desired time. His wake-up time should adjust itself accordingly.

### Ready or Not?

So . . . when is he ready to go back to sleep? You can signal him in many ways that it's time for him to sleep and not be active. By keeping the room darkened or the light subdued, by keeping ambient noise hushed (which means this isn't the time to turn on music to soothe him), by keeping your voice low, and by not playing games with him, you signal to him that it's sleep time, not awake time.

## Ⓔ *Question?*

**How can I help my baby sleep through the night?**

"Sleeping through the night" is a bit of a misnomer. We all, adults and babies alike, wake up, however briefly, at least several times during the night. If we get back to sleep quickly, when we wake up in the morning, we don't remember having awakened during the night at all. Babies, too, awaken during the night a few times. They all do. But some are "self-soothers" who can "roll over and go back to sleep." Other babies, once they wake up, cannot get themselves back to sleep and cry out. The trick with your baby isn't to get him to literally sleep through the night, but rather to get him able to go back to sleep on his own when he wakes up.

But how, when he is ready to finally go back to sleep, will he let you know? You've already learned the signals babies give when they're sleepy. Look for him to exhibit any of these signs. Maybe after being awake for two or three hours he'll get hungry, want another bottle or want to nurse again, and fall asleep while drinking. But perhaps he'll finally grow sleepy without wanting a bottle or the breast first. When he shows signs of being sleepy, put him in bed, perhaps with a pacifier if he uses one. Dependence on a pacifier for sleep is less desirable once your baby reaches the age of six or nine months. By that age, it's best if he can learn to sleep without it. You'll want to keep in mind that if a baby does fall asleep with a pacifier, he may wake up when it falls out of his mouth, and at that point, he may start crying all over again. Try to get him to sleep without it.

By putting the baby into his crib before he falls asleep, he grows used to being in the crib and falling asleep on his own. "On his own" doesn't mean totally without help. You can leave a pacifier in the crib within his reach (or even offer it to him to suck). You can also leave a cuddly, small stuffed animal in the corner of the crib or a small, light-weight blanket. Of use also is a night-light, which helps the older baby to see that there's nothing fearsome lurking. All these ideas can be your allies. But the idea is that, what-ever other help you offer him, you're not holding him until he goes to sleep in your arms or rocking him to sleep.

The earlier he reaches that level of independence, the better it is—not just for you, but also for him. Promoting sound sleeping habits early will help give him a good foun-dation for sleeping well as he grows older. Helping your baby learn to go to sleep on his own helps him get back to sleep on his own when he wakens during the night.

## Desperation Measures

Naturally, if your baby just won't or can't fall asleep unaided, it's better to help him in any reasonable way you can rather than to listen to him cry and scream all night. Work toward a goal of getting your baby to fall asleep without you helping him by following the advice here as much as possible, and you'll find that you have fewer reasons to resort to the desperation measures, such as taking him on a middle-of-the-night car drive 'round and 'round the block to let the motion of the car soothe the baby to sleep.

Perhaps if he's colicky and needs extra soothing or for some other reason is having a bad night, you'll have no choice but to hold him and rock him and sing to him. But don't make a habit of it. You want him to learn how to fall asleep at night on his own, and you want him to learn to be able to fall back to sleep on his own when he wakes in the middle of the night. The child who has not learned the former skill will never acquire the latter one.

## ⓔ *Alert!*

Don't let your baby fall asleep with a bottle. It's best if he can learn to fall asleep without it, which will aid him in learning to go back to sleep without outside help when he wakens during the night. In addition to poor sleep habits, falling asleep with a bottle can lead to problems such as cavities and ear infections.

## And So to Bed

Whether you do or don't tell your baby a fairy tale or a "her-story" or "him-story," whether you do or don't sing to her, or whether you do or don't say a prayer or read from a book of poetry, be sure to hold her and snuggle her before you put her in her crib. You can even give her a back rub. Babies love back rubs as much as older kids do, as long as you remember to be gentle. Your touch on her back not only soothes her, but also helps her bond with you and helps you bond with her. For that matter, any type of good touch will soothe her, whether it's a back rub, an actual massage, or simply your fingers lightly stroking her arm or briefly running through her hair (or over her nearly bald head). Then give her a kiss good night. After that, it's time to say "Good night, sweet dreams," and leave.

Whether or not he cooperates every night, he'll understand that it's now bedtime. He'll be soothed by your voice. He'll be lulled and comforted by the familiar bedtime routine he's slowly coming to recognize.

## Chapter 5

# Soothing Baby to Sleep

Babies and older children, too, like routines because children like what's familiar. Having a regular routine at bedtime is a comfort to a child of any age, including infants. Anything that comforts soothes, and anything that soothes can help a person, including a baby, get to sleep. But there are other ways to soothe your baby besides the bedtime routine. These may be particularly useful on those nights when your baby just can't seem to get to sleep.

## Calming Your Crying Baby

Suppose you are facing two problems: The baby is awake, and the baby is crying. This may seem to be one situation. It isn't; it's two. If it was daytime and your baby was awake, this wouldn't be a problem unless he was crying. Because it's night and you want to sleep yourself, her being awake is keeping you awake.

### Ⓔ *Alert!*

Occasionally a baby's crying can upset a parent, especially a sleepless one, to the point that a parent will lose self-control and do something to jeopardize the baby's well-being. If you feel yourself at the breaking point, hand the baby off to your spouse or simply put the baby back in his crib. He will not harm himself by crying or screaming alone in his crib for a few minutes while you get control of yourself. Under those circumstances, he is better off screaming on his own without being comforted than being at risk with a parent who is reacting emotionally.

Until your baby is ready to go back to sleep, your best effort should be to try to calm her down if she's crying so that, though she's awake and keeping you awake, at least she's not fussing or screeching. If you can calm her down, perhaps your spouse and other children can get back to sleep, even if you can't. If the baby's still up after a while, you can wake your spouse and let him or her take the next shift while you get a little sleep. But as you hold her, rock her, or otherwise soothe her and perhaps eventually feed her again, if she's awake long enough for that, be alert for a signal that she's ready to go back to sleep.

But how do you calm down a crying baby? There are a number of things you can try that will soothe and relax your little one so she is ready to fall asleep.

## Rocking and Soothing Motion Techniques

Does "the hand that rocks the cradle rule the world"? Certainly Mom rules Baby's world, though at times not as firmly as she'd like to . . . such as the times when Baby refuses to go to sleep. The word "refuses," though it's the word that is often used, is really a misnomer. Your baby isn't being willful and stubborn, no matter how much it may seem that way. More likely he's unable to go to sleep, whether because he's not sleepy or for some other reason.

If you're putting your baby in for a nap, for the night, or to go back to sleep in the middle of the night, if he simply isn't sleepy, you're swimming upstream. But if he's sleepy and just can't seem to go to sleep, there are things you can do to help, and one of those tricks, long known to parents everywhere, is to rock him.

### Rock-a-bye Baby

Many babies, in fact, naturally rock themselves. They move their bodies back and forth in rhythmic rocking motions as an apparent means of calming themselves to sleep. Some babies even do this in their sleep. (Some also bang their heads deliberately against the headboard or side of the crib at the same time as they are rocking themselves.) This bears out the value of rocking a child to sleep, a technique parents through the ages have borne witness to.

This rhythmic rocking some babies engage in, though it may be associated in some cases with medical problems (e.g., autism), is in most cases not in any way a symptom of any sort of medical problem. Most babies who engage in this type of rocking behavior are perfectly normal. So don't be alarmed if you witness your child engaging in rocking in her crib or at other times when she is tired.

## Fact

In some cultures, parents have historically carried their babies against their bodies, held in slings, a practice adopted by many moms and dads in the United States. It permits Mom to move about from place to place and keep Baby with her and allows Baby to always feel Mom close by. Even better, the motion of Mom's body as she moves about provides a natural rocking effect for Baby, which helps soothe her and aids her to sleep.

Don't feel a need to stop her, though you should remove any hard or sharp objects (sharp objects don't belong in a crib) that she might hurt herself on by rocking against or banging her head against them. Safely padding the place where she bangs her head is advisable, too. In most cases of babies rocking themselves, the child out-grows the behavior naturally by age two.

### This Furniture Rocks!

Babies in centuries past were more often put to bed in cradles than in cribs, at least in their infancy. Cradles sit on rockers rather than on steady legs, and parents can rock their baby to sleep in his cradle as he lies there. Though cradles are still in limited use, they have fallen out of favor in comparison with their usage in previous centuries.

Rocking chairs, though not as popular as they used to be, are used both in general and, more specifically, by parents. A parent who wants to soothe a baby with a rocking motion, yet is tired of pacing the floor, can sit in the chair, rock, and soothe the baby while she herself is comfortably seated and relaxed. The motion of the chair can help soothe your frayed nerves, too, if your baby has been crying incessantly or has gotten you out of bed in the middle of the night.

### Car Rides as Soothers

Car rides are a well-known means of soothing a baby to sleep. Many a baby has taken a nap at an unfortunate time because he fell asleep during a drive, and many parents have, in desperation, gotten into the car in the middle of the night and taken a drive to nowhere with the hope that the car ride would get the baby to sleep when all else failed.

The main disadvantage to using the motion of the car as a soother is that the baby may become dependent on the motion of the car in order to get to sleep. Ideally, you don't even want him to become dependent on being rocked to sleep in a cradle or a rocker. Neither do you want him to become dependent on being held in your arms as you walk the floor, perhaps with you lightly bouncing him as you pace. But if, for a while, you have to rock him in one of these manners, that's not too much of a hardship on you. Driving him around in the car every time he wakes up during the night is not a position you want to be in!

You could be taking two or three drives every night, and what do you do in freezing weather, when Baby is dressed only in pajamas? (Suppose you put a snowsuit on him. When he falls asleep in the car in his snowsuit, do you put him back in the crib, snowsuit and all, or undress him and wake him up again?) A car ride as a soother may be a last-ditch desperation measure when you're at your wits' end, but don't rely on it.

## Ⓔ *Alert!*

The main downside to getting your baby to sleep by putting him in his swing is simply that you want him to learn to fall asleep in his crib without the aid of anything more than a teddy bear (for an older baby) or perhaps a pacifier (for a younger infant). If he becomes dependent on the swing, he'll be waking you up every time he wakes during the night and, unable to get back to sleep without the swinging motion, become frustrated and cry.

### The Swing as Soother

Baby swings are another device that can lull babies to sleep readily. Again, it's preferable not to get your baby dependent on swinging in order to get him to sleep, although the same problems inherent in car drives are not present in putting your baby in the swing.

Besides the fact that you don't want your baby to become dependent on the swing in order to fall asleep, there is one other disadvantage. If he falls asleep in the swing, his head is likely to loll to the side or forward, and he could wake up with a stiff neck unless you remove him from the swing and put him in his crib—at which point there's a good chance he'll wake up again.

### Other Rocking Devices

Your baby's carriage is another device that imparts a rocking motion. Though the rocking isn't as pronounced as that from a cradle or rocking chair, a swing, or even a car, there's a definite soothing sense of motion, and plenty of babies who don't seem able to nap indoors have fallen asleep in their carriages, pushed along outdoors by their moms (and aided by being out in the fresh air).

There are also bouncing chairs that your baby can sit in and bounce or be bounced in. Though she's less likely to sleep in one of these, it's not unheard of, and even if she doesn't fall asleep in the chair, the motion may soothe her sufficiently that when you transfer her from the chair to her crib, she'll be able to drift off to sleep.

## *Singing and Talking*

A few more words here about a subject we've already discussed in connection with your baby's bedtime routine: your voice. It's a real soother. Though lullabies are great, just talking to your baby can calm and relax him, too.

 **Fact**

Any soothing voice will help calm and relax your baby, but Mom's voice or Dad's voice is especially powerful in its ability to help soothe Baby. The familiar tones of her Mommy or Daddy's voice are especially welcome, more so than recorded music, even by someone who's a far better singer than you are.

### Watch That Tone

You have to be mindful of your tone of voice. Were you harried and hassled and running late this afternoon because the baby wouldn't stop crying or your toddler kept getting into mischief? Have you just rushed through what should have been a half hour of dinner preparation in barely fifteen minutes, trying to get dinner started early enough so that you wouldn't wind up eating at 9:00 P.M.? Did you just have to hang up on three telemarketers in a row, all of whom caught you at a very frazzled and frenzied juncture of your day? Are you now in a hurry to get back to the kitchen before the water for the potatoes boils over?

Take a deep breath and calm down before you start talking to your baby, or your voice won't be soothing at all!

Your voice has a powerful ability to calm and gentle your baby, but only if you sound calm and gentle yourself. If you've been rushing, feel harried, or are having a bad time of it, you're going to reflect it in the tone of your voice.

### Your Repertoire

Once you've gotten control of yourself and you know your voice is going to sound calm and soothing, you can talk to your baby, sing to her, or do both. If you're talking, it doesn't much matter what you say. You can reiterate the events of the day, as long as it hasn't been a bad day. If it has been a bad day, you're likely to start sounding agitated as you recount the day's happenings. Why not tell her a story that makes you happy, maybe the story of the day you met her dad or some other story that will put a glow (but not excitement) in your voice? You can even recite a list of stations on the local train line or the grocery list, as long as you speak it in a soft, soothing tone.

If you're singing, any quiet, slow song will do. It doesn't have to be an actual lullaby. You can sing *Twinkle, Twinkle, Little Star, The Bear Went over the Mountain,* or another folk song; any soft, slow, popular song you know; or almost anything else with the right slow tempo. Many hymns are slow and soothing. You can even sing her a commercial jingle or TV theme song, if the tempo is right. The words aren't what's important. It's the slow tempo and the sound of your voice that count. You do not have to have operatic-quality vocal cords. You can even go off tune, and your baby won't know the difference. Just don't screech.

## A Cry for Attention

Sometimes a baby cries for no apparent reason. She simply is awake, can't go back to sleep, and wants to be held or for you to pay attention to her. You can try holding her, cuddling her, rocking her, or singing to her. But if you want to try putting her back into her crib by herself, offer her one of these:

- A "blankie" (soft, cuddly blanket she can hold)
- A warm blanket
- A "lovey" (soft, cuddly toy)
- A pacifier (or "binky")

She may go back to sleep or at least remain quiet though awake for a while. After all, it's not important that she sleeps at that moment, as long as you and the rest of your family can get your sleep.

### Ⓔ *Alert!*

Never warm a blanket by placing it on a radiator or in the microwave. It creates a fire hazard, as well as posing a danger to your baby if the blanket develops hot spots, especially when warmed in the microwave.

## Swaddling

Some infants are happiest when they're swaddled; some hate the confinement. Why not experiment and see if your baby enjoys being wrapped in a receiving blanket?

Having recently emerged from the confining atmosphere of the womb, some babies feel more secure when they're wrapped from the shoulders down in a light blanket.

## E Alert!

Never swaddle your baby if the room she sleeps in is warm. SIDS has been associated with overheating, so either lower the temperature in the room or don't swaddle her.

How to swaddle your baby:

- Lay a blanket on Baby's crib or another flat surface and fold down the top right corner about six inches.
- Place Baby on her back with her head on top of the fold.
- Pull the corner near Baby's left hand across her body.
- Tuck that corner under Baby's back on the right side, under her arm.
- Pull the bottom corner up till it is under Baby's chin.
- Bring the loose corner over Baby's right arm and tuck it under the back on her side.
- Alternatively, if your baby likes having her arms free, swaddle her under the arms so that she has access to her hands and fingers.

Special swaddling blankets are available. If you do swaddle your baby, take care that no part of her face is covered. Once your baby is beginning to move about, you should stop swaddling her, since she can become entangled in the blanket.

## Massage

When your baby was in your womb, he was in constant contact with his surroundings. It was almost like getting an all-over massage at all times. Any time he moved, he got rubbed.

Now that he's out in the great big world, he probably misses that sense of being touched all over. Most people of any age enjoy gentle, loving touch. Why wouldn't your baby enjoy it just as much? Your touch on his skin communicates love and also gives him the light rubbing that he had become used to receiving in your womb. Massage serves at least three purposes:

- It communicates love and caring.
- It soothes and gentles him, helping him relax so he can sleep.
- It's an old remedy for colic.

### Ⓔ Essential

Before massaging your baby, be sure to remove any jewelry that might scratch or rub him. Take off rings, bracelets, or anything at all that could pinch his skin or inflict any other sort of pain. Even a totally smooth wedding ring might catch his soft skin and pinch him.

When massaging your baby, remember that he's small and delicate; you can't use the same type of touch you use on your spouse or friends or even on a child of five or ten. Use oil (it can be baby oil, or something like almond oil, or even olive oil), which you may warm lightly (take care with the temperature) if you wish. Rub it into your hands before you massage Baby.

Cover your baby with a towel (except for his face, of course), exposing each part of his body as you massage it and then covering it up again. You might want to start with his feet, one at a time, working your way up to his legs and then massage his arms, the back of his neck, his back, and finally his tummy. When massaging his tummy, use clockwise, circular strokes. (Don't be surprised if this maneuver impels him to pass gas or even poop.) If he begins to protest, to squirm, to grow restless, or to cry, either you're stroking him too hard, you've pinched him, or you've stayed too long in one spot. Try massaging a different part of him.

Not only massage but other types of touch also feel good to your baby. A light, tickly sort of touch is one that many babies enjoy, and so is a featherlight stroke, which is similar.

## Quiet Games

Though bedtime isn't a time for games—you want your baby to understand that it's time to sleep, not to play—the bedtime routine or any other time when you want to interact with Baby and have quiet fun with her is a good time for the relaxing fun of quiet games.

You can play one of the traditional games, such as "Where Is Thumbkin?" or "Here Is the Church, Here Is the Steeple," or you can make up one of your own. Quiet games are just that: quiet, relaxing games that won't get Baby revved up. If this is a prebed or prenap game or a game at any time when you want Baby to relax, then it isn't the time for hiding below her vision level and popping up and saying "Ah," "Boo," or any other such excitement. Even a demure version of "Peek-a-Boo" with you merely holding your hands up in front of your face or hers to block her vision of your face is inappropriate here.

## Ⓔ *Alert!*

Mobiles are popular with babies and their parents, and indeed they keep many a baby amused in his crib. Though watching a mobile may keep your baby entertained quietly until he falls asleep and watching it may be hypnogogic (sleep-inducing), you don't want the baby to get accustomed to having the mobile going 'round and 'round. If he isn't yet asleep by the time the mobile has run down, he's likely to start crying until you come in and rewind it.

### Tactics to Avoid

It's preferable that your baby fall asleep in her own crib rather than in another spot. There are parents who lie down next to their babies on their own beds and snuggle the baby till she falls asleep and then transfer her to her crib. Some parents put their babies to sleep on a sheet, quilt, or other surface in the middle of the living room or even the kitchen so that the baby can see Mom or Dad cooking or reading or the family watching TV while she goes to sleep.

A baby who falls asleep on Mom's bed, lying next to Mom, may be reassured that Mom is nearby and may indeed fall asleep more quickly, but she isn't learning to go to sleep independently. A baby who falls asleep in the midst of the family hubbub is learning not to let sound and light disturb her, but she isn't learning to associate sleep with darkness and relative quiet. She too isn't learning to go to sleep independently.

Just as you don't really want to run in every couple of minutes to rewind your baby's mobile (and this is especially true at 1:00 A.M.), the same principle applies to playing music in your baby's room. It's great by day, but don't rely on music to put him to sleep at night. Your baby may fall asleep to the music and then wake up when the music goes off. You don't want to have to keep running into his room to turn the music back on every hour!

The best place for your baby to fall asleep is in her own crib (or bassinet), not on the floor, not on your bed (unless you are cosleeping, see Chapter 8), and not in your arms. Once she's reached the age of about six weeks, try to get her used to going to sleep in her crib. It will not only get her accustomed to going to sleep in her own bed at bedtime in the months and years ahead, but it will also aid her in getting accustomed to settling herself down to sleep so that when she wakes in the middle of the night she can resettle herself without awakening you.

## Chapter 6

# Sound and Light

From what you know so far, you might think that the best thing for helping your baby to sleep well is to always put him to bed in a quiet, dark room with as little light and noise and other distractions as possible. As a general rule, your baby is likely to sleep better when there's no noise or light to bother him, but you know that generalities are just that—generally true—and don't hold true 100 percent of the time.

## *How Babies React to Sound*

When babies are first born, they can sleep through noise, bright light, and all manner of other circumstances that would surely awaken you if you were the one trying to sleep. Though your baby is peripherally aware of the things going on around her, she tends not to react to them at first.

As your baby grows older and more aware of the world around her, she'll become more attuned to the things going on in the room she's in, as well as sounds coming from beyond her room. She'll learn to recognize your voice, she'll grow interested in what people around her are doing (even though she doesn't yet comprehend the meaning or purpose of most of what she sees), and she'll become more alert and more aware overall.

 **Fact**

You can take comfort if your baby is a few months old and had learned to resettle herself back to sleep but now is waking again and calling for you. Know that she may just be going through a phase of becoming more aware of and interested in the world and that after a couple of weeks or so, she'll probably learn to resettle herself again when she wakes, unless she hears or sees something she finds alarming or scary.

As all these changes take place within her, she'll also become more easily awakened as well as more easily distracted from going to sleep. What was that noise? Is something interesting going on in the other room that she's missing? Was that Mommy's voice? Why isn't Mommy in here with her? Of course, she can't literally think these thoughts in so many words, but in a rudimentary way, such thoughts do occur to her.

As well, when she wakes up in the middle of the night, even if she has previously learned to resettle herself and get back to sleep on her own, she may now find that there are too many interesting sights and sounds clamoring for her attention. Any of these might catch her eye or ear and prevent her from going back to sleep:

- The sound of someone snoring in the same room or snoring loudly in a nearby room
- The sound of a bed creaking as someone rolls over in his or her sleep
- The sound of a plane going by overhead or a bus or car going by outside
- The clank or hiss of a radiator or the sound of an air conditioner cycling on
- The sound of a TV or radio playing in another room loudly enough for her to hear
- The audible murmur of voices as you and your spouse hold a conversation
- The slam of the neighbors' door
- The sound of people talking in the street
- The footsteps of the neighbors in the upstairs apartment or the stereo or TV of the neighbors downstairs
- The buzz of a fly or mosquito

As she becomes more aware of the world around her, everything catches her interest—even at midnight or three in the morning.

It's impossible to screen out all the noises and sounds of the world, unless you were to put your baby to bed in a windowless, soundproof room. But that's absurd, and it's not desirable, either. What will she do when she gets older, and what will you do if you travel with her?

## Getting Baby Used to Distractions

Putting your baby to bed in a dark, silent room seems like a good thing for helping her to go to sleep and stay asleep. As discussed earlier, putting her to bed in a quiet, darkened room signals to her that it's time to go to sleep. But actually there's a paradox at work here: If you expect your baby to sleep in the midst of all the light and sound and activity of a bustling house, she's going to have an increasingly tough time of it as she gets older. If you put her in for nighttime sleep and for naps in a totally darkened, totally hushed atmosphere, the first time there's a disruption of this pattern or at least the first time she's old enough to be aware of the sounds and hubbub, she's not going to handle it very well.

Of course, the degree of quiet your baby will get used to depends to a great extent on the layout of your house and the circumstances of your life.

- Do you live in an apartment or a one-story house, where the baby's room (whether he has his own room or sleeps in yours or shares with a sibling) is near everything else or is his room upstairs and away from the noise of much of your day-to-day living?

- Do you have one or more other kids, who are likely to be noisy at times when the baby is supposed to be sleeping?
- Do you have a resident grandparent or other relative living with you?
- Do you live on a quiet street, or is there a lot of street noise?
- Do you have noisy neighbors or quiet ones?

New circumstances can suddenly bring an unaccustomed level of noise or a change in light conditions to your baby's room. They include:

- A member of the family moving in with you
- A houseguest coming for a visit
- Your other child, whose room your baby shares, is sick in bed and confined to the room and doing a lot of sneezing, coughing, and calling loudly and often for you
- Holding a party or other gathering at which there are noisy guests or simply enough guests to raise the noise level
- Construction or other noisy work taking place outside your house or in the apartment of a neighbor during the baby's nap hours or possibly still ongoing at the hour when he would normally go to bed for the night
- Moving to a new home, where the ambient noise level is louder or even where the noises are simply different

- Going away on vacation as a family and keeping the baby in your room while you are traveling, or having him stay in his cousin's room while you're visiting your sister, or simply having new noises or a different noise level and different things to look at as he stays in a room all by himself while you're visiting at Grandma's

There is no one easy solution to the problem. There are, however, a few things you can do to minimize the hassle.

## *Naptime Is for Learning*

You can minimize noises and light at your baby's naptime without making the room pitch black and completely silent. This topic is covered in more detail in Chapter 10. But for now, here's what you should know: If your baby learns to nap with the door of her room open and with everyday life and its everyday noise going on in the house beyond her room, she will be more able to tolerate noise when she sleeps as a general rule. You may not want to run the vacuum cleaner while she naps or sleeps, and you may want to avoid doing anything that creates a sudden loud noise, such as hammering or giving your two-year-old child a pot and a wooden spoon to play with when your baby is napping.

But you don't have to keep the noise level in the house in a total hush. You can certainly keep the stereo or TV on in another room at a reasonable volume. You can talk on the phone or chit-chat with someone who's there with you in the house. You can use a sewing machine, blender, or food processor. You can run the clothes washer and dryer or the dishwasher.

Ⓔ *Essential*

> If an older child shares a room with the baby, this older child doesn't need to give up the room for the baby's exclusive use during hours when the baby is sleeping, but certain accommodations are helpful. For example, the use of a strong, bright reading light, which directs its glow in a concentrated area, can help illuminate one patch of the carpet on which the older child is playing, while the rest of the room is darkened. If the older child is of school age, use the reading light to illuminate his homework as he works on it at his desk or table.

## Life Goes on While Baby Naps

In other words, you can see to it that life goes on around the sleeping baby, complete with the noises that living brings, as long as you don't encourage activities that create unduly loud or suddenly escalating noises. In this way, the baby doesn't get accustomed to absolute silence and darkness when she naps. She won't grow to need such conditions in order to fall asleep for her nap and stay asleep for the length of her usual naptime. Learning to nap with some noise and some light present will help accustom her to sleeping in those conditions at any time, so that even at night she'll be able to sleep with some noise going on around her. This is particularly helpful if you have the baby sleeping in your room, but even more important, it will serve you well not only now, but also over the years ahead, as your child grows.

If you have an upcoming vacation or move or you are expecting some other change in lifestyle that will affect the level of noise in the baby's surroundings, you can gradually acclimate her in advance during naptimes. Turn up the volume of the stereo in the living room or your room a bit from the usual level. Speak a little louder when you're on the phone or have a friend over during the baby's nap. Get the baby used to a greater level of noise.

### Acclimating Baby to Light

If you expect increased light to be a factor in the upcoming change, leave the baby's blinds opened just a little more than usual. Let her get used to napping in a room that's just a little less dark than she's been used to normally.

Don't make these changes radical. Change them gradually: a little more light and noise today, just a bit more tomorrow, and still more the next day. By the time the visitors come, or you leave on your vacation, or the construction starts down the street, or you've moved to your new house, your baby should be ready for the change in ambient noise level and light level, if that's a factor, too.

### As Baby Grows More Aware

Of course, the problem is not always related to something external such as a visitor or pending move. Sometimes the problem arises without any change in your lifestyle. The change, in this case, is internal: Your baby is growing older, more aware of what is going on around him and more interested in all the activity. The same baby who could sleep through a thunderstorm right overhead at age one month now wakes up merely because the cat walked into the baby's room and meowed, or your baby can no longer get to sleep when people are talking in the living room, even though everyone is speaking in a hushed voice, although last month this was no problem.

Newborns cannot form the thought, "I wonder what I'm missing?" However, an older baby who hears conversation, laughter, and other "people noises" will sometimes feel he's missing out on something fun. Wondering what's going on elsewhere in the house, he will be reluctant to go to sleep or go back to sleep. He wants to be part of the action.

## *Quiet versus Loud*

Though noise won't bother most newborns, "most" is not the same as "all," and even some newborns will find it difficult to go to sleep or go back to sleep if there is loud noise occurring in the house.

You already know that older babies will react to the noises around them. This is particularly true of babies who have been allowed to become accustomed to silence during nighttime and naptime. This is also particularly true of intermittent noises or noises that are variable in volume. That is, a consistently loud stereo or TV or consistently loud conversation is less troubling than is a noise that occurs, stops, and recurs after a pause or a noise that rises in volume, lowers, and rises again.

When your baby is sleeping, try to minimize noises that change volume abruptly or that recur intermittently. They are the most disturbing.

## Dark versus Light

For the baby who is used to sleeping in near darkness or even total darkness, suddenly being expected to sleep with light entering the room may cause a problem. This condition can occur in any number of situations. Here are just a few:

- You have moved the baby from your room to his brother's room, and his brother keeps the light on when he's in the room, though you managed to refrain from doing so when the baby was sleeping in your room.
- You have moved from one house or apartment to another, and the hallway light now shines into the baby's room, which wasn't the situation in your last home.
- You are on vacation at Grandma's, in a hotel, or otherwise, and the lighting conditions are different.
- The baby was born in winter, but now it stays light out much later, and his blinds or shades aren't adequate for the job of keeping daylight out at bedtime.

On the other hand, the problem may be absence of light. "But my baby never minded darkness before," you say. True, but your baby is one week older, one month older, or several months older and more aware of what's going on around him, more able to form thoughts, and more likely to be scared by "what's lurking under the bed" or other fears. At the same time you make sure there isn't too much light for your baby's physical comfort, make sure there is enough light for his emotional comfort.

## Ⓔ *Essential*

In the half hour or so before you put your baby to bed, it's time to start setting the stage. Now is a good time to try to avoid very bright lights around him, as well as very loud or fast and rhythmic music. Now is a time for not only quiet bonding, but also soft lights, and if your household is one in which you generally keep music playing, now is a time for quiet music, too.

Also make sure that what he sees won't upset him. Here are some of the sights that might trigger fear or concern in your baby:

- The sight of your family's cat jumping up onto a nearby piece of furniture, barely visible in the semidarkness and not understandable to Baby. (A night-light would help.)
- Shifting shapes on the wall as the curtain on her window flutters in the breeze, its moving shadow created by the streetlight. (Install blinds or a shade, or buy a heavier curtain.)
- The shadow of a branch outside her window moving eerily on the wall. (Block the shadow with a shade, curtain, or blind.)

## *Using Sound Machines*

Sometimes the presence of ambient sound is unavoidable. This is true if you have noisy neighbors, if construction is going on nearby, and in various other circumstances. The answer to this dilemma often is white sound (also known as white noise). White sound is a constant noise of even volume, which is loud enough to either drown out or at least muffle other ambient sounds, yet is not so loud as to be disturbing of itself.

 **Fact**

> You can buy a white sound machine to put in your baby's room to drown out ambient noise. Try looking in an electronics store, a department store, or a large store that caters to babies' needs. But you can also create white sound with devices you already have. Any machine that creates a steady noise that will drown out other noises is a candidate for a makeshift white noise device.

Have you ever had a bathroom faucet develop an annoying drip in the middle of the night? The intermittent sound was enough to keep you awake, yet you weren't going to try to repair it yourself at 3:00 A.M. Did you turn on a fan to cover up the noise of the drip? If you did, you were employing white sound. The steady, constant whirring of a fan, far from being annoying, is lulling, but more to the point, it drowns out or minimizes other noises around you.

Manufacturers have created devices known as white sound machines for the specific purpose of creating a steady, low-volume noise to minimize other distracting noises. Most are sold to facilitate sleep, though some people use them for other purposes. (One such use is to aid a person who is trying to study or work while distracting noises or conversations are going on in his vicinity.)

When it comes to the use of other devices as make-shift white sound machines, fans and air conditioners are probably the most popular, though vaporizers are used by many people, too. Some people find that a radio set at a low volume and tuned to a station that plays soft music serves as white noise for them or their kids. Other people tune the radio to a spot between stations so that the radio either emits a hum or buzzes with static, which creates an acceptable white noise for them. You may have some other device in your home that would create an acceptable type of white noise. Do you still have an old electric typewriter, and does it hum fairly loudly when you turn the switch on? You may never use it for typing again, but it might be just the white sound machine you need to drown out the sounds of your household or your neighborhood and help your baby to sleep.

Some clock radios can play "nature sounds," or you can also look for audiotapes and CDs of noises that serve as white sound. There are recordings of gentle surf, the breeze in the trees, and soft birdcalls—all of them supposedly lulling, soothing noises that mask the ambient noises that might disturb a sleeper. If your baby has a stereo in her room, you can play one of these tapes or CDs on the stereo. At the end of the tape or CD, the white sound will stop, but by then, your child should be asleep.

Should she wake in the middle of the night and need the sound to help her get back to sleep, you can always put it on again. (If she doesn't have a stereo in her room, you can buy an inexpensive, portable cassette player at your local electronics store.)

## Ⓔ *Essential*

> If you use an air conditioner, humidifier, or even a fan, check the room periodically to see if temperature, humidity, or drafts are becoming uncomfortable to your baby.

Of course, no amount of white noise will cover a screaming two-year-old having a tantrum in your baby's doorway, or a smoke alarm in the hallway just outside the baby's room signaling that the popcorn has burned, or an ambulance rushing to your next-door neighbor's house with its siren wailing at full blast. But white noise is an aid when you have friends over for the evening and want to laugh unrestrainedly, when the dog barks at something he sees out the window, and perhaps even when you want to run the vacuum cleaner.

The downside to white sound and the reason some people advise against it is that once you get your baby dependent on this steady background for easy sleeping, it will be hard for her to sleep without it. Accustomed to the steady drone, shush or hum of the fan, vaporizer, typewriter, white sound machine, or other device, she will find it hard to sleep without it.

One possibility is to attempt to wean your child from the white sound by turning it off about half an hour after she goes to sleep. Assuredly she will wake up a number of times during the night, as we all do, but by then the house may be quiet enough that she doesn't require the sound of the white sound machine in the background in order to get herself back to sleep.

# Chapter 7

# The Proper Nursery

To help your baby to sleep well, you need to furnish the nursery with well-thought-out "tools" for sleep—a proper bed (crib or cradle) to sleep in and the right bedding and clothing, all with an eye for comfort and safety. We've all heard the expression, "He's safe in bed." But how safe is your baby in bed, and how well will he sleep there?

## *Choosing the Right Crib*

Your baby's crib should have the firmest mattress available. Smothering has been implicated in cases of crib death, and a mattress that isn't extremely firm is a mattress into which a baby's face can sink. Not only is there a risk of your baby getting his nostrils pressed against the mattress once he is old enough to roll over (remember to always put baby to sleep on his back), but there is also the danger that, with his nose into a soft mattress, he could keep breathing but breathe his own exhaled carbon dioxide over and over and not get much oxygen. In this situation, he could become dopey and not have the strength to cry or struggle for air. This is a mortal hazard.

If your crib is a hand-me-down, either from your own previous child or from a friend's child, invest the money to buy a new mattress for it. It's well worth the cost.

## Ⓔ *Alert!*

Never use a waterbed for your baby's bed. Waterbeds simply aren't firm enough for a baby, and if he rolls over onto his tummy, he could get smothered in the softness. A baby cosleeping in a family bed should not be sleeping on a waterbed, either. Stick with a conventional mattress.

Besides being sure that the crib's mattress is firm enough, you also need to be sure that it fits tight to the side of the crib. You should not be able to fit more than two fingers between the mattress and the side of the crib.

The slats of the crib should be no more than 2⅜ inches apart, as a precaution against your baby putting his head between the slats and getting wedged or strangled. Be sure there are no loose, missing, or broken slats or hardware. There should be no corner posts over 1/16 inch high and no cutout designs in the headboard or footboard.

### Painted Cribs

Be sure that there is no paint flaking from the crib. This is primarily a hazard with old cribs, but if you're using a family heirloom or a thrift store purchase, you need to be alert for this hazard. If this is a family heirloom or other older crib and it's painted, make very sure it's not painted with lead-based paint. If you're not able to verify that the crib was manufactured in the post lead-based paint era and it does have paint on it, be safe and strip the paint off and then repaint it.

Generally, lead-based paint should be suspected in any crib dating back to the 1970s or earlier, but there is no hard-and-fast rule. A crib dating from the 1980s could have been repainted with lead-based paint by someone who had a can of it lying around and was unaware of the danger. If you must use an old crib, have a sample of the paint tested first.

Though family heirlooms have great sentimental value, you're safest with a new crib in great condition. If you're looking to buy a crib at a thrift store to save some money, by the time you buy a new mattress and new bumpers and you strip off any suspect paint and repaint the crib, you won't have saved that much money. So consider just investing in the safety and security of a new crib.

Another hazard to watch out for is decorative knobs or other decorative fixtures that stick out from the crib itself. Once your baby learns to stand, he is at risk from any decorative fixture on the crib that might poke his eye, come loose and be swallowed, or present any other hazard, such as rough edges on which he can cut or scrape himself.

**Ⓔ Essential**

With your crib—as with all equipment you have for Baby—be on the lookout for recall announcements. If your baby's crib, high chair, stroller, playpen, or any other equipment is recalled, return it at once. Don't say, "Oh, it seems fine. We haven't had any trouble so far." Don't take risks with your baby's life or well-being. You can check the following Web site for information on recalls: ✎ *www.cpsc.gov.*

There's a lot to be aware of in buying a crib (or in accepting a hand-me-down crib). Most recently manufactured cribs conform to the necessary safety measures, but it pays to be a wary consumer even if you're buying a new crib. With an old crib, especially a family heirloom (your family's or someone else's) that's been around for a while, there's a greater chance that not all safety precautions were observed.

If your crib is mesh-sided, the Consumer Products Safety Council recommends the following precautions, which also apply to mesh-sided playpens:

- Mesh less than ¼ inch in size, smaller than the tiny buttons on a baby's clothing
- Mesh with no tears, holes, or loose threads that could entangle a baby
- Mesh securely attached to top rail and floor plane
- Top rail cover with no tears or holes
- Staples are not missing, loose, or exposed

## ⓔ *Alert!*

Be sure that the crib you select does not have the latches for the side rails in a place where your baby can reach them from within the crib. You don't want him to be able to engineer his escape from the confines of the crib.

### Using a Portable Crib

If you use a portable crib, observe the following precautions in addition to those for regular cribs:

- Be sure that there are no tears in the mesh fabric sides.
- Be sure the mattress pad is no thicker than 1 inch.
- Do not use an additional mattress or padding. Infants can get tangled up in extra padding and suffocate.
- Never leave your baby in the portable crib with a side folded down. Even if he's not old enough to crawl out,

he could roll into the space between the mattress and the mesh and become trapped.

- Be sure the latches on the crib are in place and locked to prevent the crib from collapsing.
- Be sure no screws, rivets, wing nuts, or other hardware are sticking out of the crib.

## Choosing a Cradle

If your baby is to sleep in a cradle, the same safety precautions apply as those we discussed regarding cribs. The mattress needs to be extremely firm; if the cradle has slats rather than solid sides, they should be no more than 2⅜ inches apart; and you should not be able to fit more than two fingers between the mattress and the side of the cradle. In addition, once the baby is able to stand, he should be moved to a crib for safety's sake.

The main advantage to a cradle is that the baby can be rocked while in bed. But cradles, being nearer to the floor, are more vulnerable to drafts. They are easier for your family pet to access; so if you don't want your cat jumping into the cradle or your dog putting her paws up on the cradle, leaning over, and licking your baby's face, you might want to use a crib instead of a cradle for your baby. These same concerns apply to bassinets. The bassinet should not be placed on top of another piece of furniture, which is hazardous and not recommended due to the danger of tipping and falling. In fact, once a baby is active, he should not be sleeping in a bassinet at all. Follow the manufacturer's guidelines as to the age and weight at which your baby should stop sleeping in the bassinet.

Tips for using a bassinet safely:

- Be sure your baby's bassinet has a wide, stable base and sturdy bottom.
- Be sure the spaces between spindles or rails are no larger than 2⅜ inches (the same as for cribs).
- Check screws and bolts for tightness, not only when you first buy the bassinet, but periodically thereafter.
- If the bassinet has collapsible legs for storage purposes, be sure the locks on them are in good working order so that the legs don't collapse while Baby is in the bassinet.
- Be sure any decorative bows or ribbons are out of Baby's reach and trimmed short and stitched securely for extra safety.

## Taking Safety Precautions

There are a few other things in your baby's nursery that you should use in the proper way to avoid creating a dangerous situation for your baby.

### Crib Bumper Pads

Some parents feel that their baby is safer in a crib that has bumper pads. These pads serve two useful purposes. First, they prevent a very young and tiny infant from sticking her head between the slats of the crib, though this should not be an issue if the slats are not farther apart than the recommended 2⅜ inches. Their second purpose is cushioning your baby's head from the hard wood in the event that, once she is old enough to roll over, she does so and hits her head against the sides of the crib. They also help cushion her head in the event that she starts rocking herself and bangs her head against the nearest surface.

Bumper pads, however, present their own set of hazards. To begin with, if you use them, make sure they are tied to the crib slats at each corner and in the middle. Also, make sure that there are no strings hanging down from them that your baby could swallow or in which her fingers or toes could get caught.

 **Alert!**

> Be sure to check the condition of your baby's crib bumper pads regularly to be sure the vinyl or other covering material remains intact. Poorly manufactured bumper pads can crack or rip, leaving your baby able to get at the stuffing inside.

As soon as your baby is old enough to get on her hands and knees, remove the bumper pads. Otherwise your baby might try to climb up on the bumper pads, using them as steps, in an attempt to get out of the crib by himself. So be sure to remove them before that can happen.

### Other Crib Climbing Hazards

Once your baby is old enough to pull herself up into a standing position, be sure that the crib's mattress is at the lowest possible setting, to facilitate keeping her from climbing out. It may be more awkward for you, as you'll have to bend over farther to change her diaper or clothes when she's in the crib, but either inconvenience yourself and bend or remove her from the crib when you're performing one of these tasks. Set the mattress as far down as possible to discourage climbing.

Remove your baby's mobile once she starts standing up. You don't want her pulling it down on top of her or falling in an effort to grab it. In a further effort to keep your baby from climbing out of the crib, be sure to remove all large stuffed animals from the crib. The giant teddy bear, panda, or dog may be cute, cuddly, and lovable in its hugeness, but it's also a too-handy, too-tempting stepstool for your baby. If she steps up onto it, she might be able to get over the railing and fall to the floor. She might only fall off the stuffed animal back into the crib, but you surely don't want that happening, either.

**Fact**

The biggest hazard with loose-fitting sheets is the risk of their coming untucked and winding around your baby's neck. Additionally, they might wrap around some other part of her body—most likely a hand, arm, foot, or leg. Always be sure to buy the right size sheets and keep them tucked securely.

### More Safety Precautions

Be sure the sheets on your baby's crib fit tightly. Loose sheets are a smothering hazard. Once your baby learns to roll over, he's going to spend some time sleeping on his tummy. At this stage of his development, when he's stronger and he's more able to lift his head up easily, sleeping on his tummy puts him at less of a risk for SIDS than does sleeping on his tummy when he's younger. But loose-fitting sheets leave him at risk. If he's on his tummy, face-down, and inhales into a loose-fitting sheet, the sheet can rise up with his breathing and block his nose and mouth.

In addition, be sure you keep the side rail of the crib up, securely locked, whenever your baby is in his crib except when you are changing his diaper or clothes inside his crib. When you leave your baby in his crib, keep the side rail locked in the up position. This is true even if you are just stepping over to his dresser or closet to get a clean pair of pajamas or set of clothes. It is particularly important if you're leaving the room hurriedly to answer the phone or doorbell. Take another second to snap the rail up into place first.

## Be Aware of Hazards

You should check not only when you first get the crib, but also periodically thereafter to be sure there are no loose or missing screws, bolts, or other hardware or attachments or parts of the crib. Loose or missing hardware could compromise the crib's safety and sturdiness. In addition, once your baby is crawling around on his own, if some piece of hardware falls onto the floor and if he finds a nut or bolt on the floor, there's a very good chance he'll swallow it or, worse, choke on it in an attempt to swallow it.

If you're going to hang a mobile for your baby to look at, hang it beyond the crib, not right over it, so that it cannot come loose and fall from the ceiling onto your baby.

Once your baby is old enough to stand, remove the mobile altogether. To be on the safe side, don't even wait until he's standing but remove it once he's old enough to get up on his hands and knees. This way he can't be tempted to try to climb for the mobile. This is true whether you've heeded the advice here and hung the mobile off to the side or beyond the foot of the crib or even if you've hung the mobile over the crib despite this warning.

## Ⓔ *Alert!*

If a crib mobile does fall from the ceiling and into the crib, even if it misses hitting your baby, he might cut himself on an edge, try to swallow a part of it, or hurt his eye by rolling over onto it. Don't hang mobiles directly over the crib.

## *Bedding*

A less obvious concern, but one that still bears consideration, is dirty sheets. You should change the sheet on your baby's crib frequently. Of course, you're going to change the sheet if your baby's wet diaper leaks through to the crib or if he pees while you're changing his diaper in the crib and the urine gets onto the sheet. But there might be some diaper leakage that is less evident and that dries before you have the opportunity to become aware of it.

In addition, you might not notice or be able to see dried milk stains from a bottle of milk or formula he drank in bed which leaked, perhaps because he was playing with the nipple. Then there is spit-up, which again you might not be aware of if it dries before you have a chance to see it on the sheets. The milk will sour and create unhealthy conditions, both in terms of germs and in terms of attracting insects. Change the sheets as soon as you notice any sort of stain, and change the sheets every few days even if you don't notice urine stains, milk stains, poop stains, or any other stains on the sheets.

 **Fact**

The American Academy of Pediatrics advises that "all fabrics used in your child's room—sleepwear, sheets, curtains—should be flame-retardant."

### Finding the Right Bedding

The importance of tight-fitting crib sheets has already been covered, but what should the sheets be made of? There are two schools of thought on this subject.

One school of thought holds that you should buy only flame-retardant sheets that have been specially treated. Certainly, these are a safety-conscious choice. But are they the best choice?

There is another school of thought that says they aren't, for two reasons. To begin with, flame-retardant sheets are chemically treated, and some studies have found the chemicals used to be carcinogenic. In addition, these sheets are usually made either partially or completely from artificial fibers such as polyester. Those cute decorated sheets with favorite cartoon characters or circus themes on them are certainly adorable, but read the label: What are they made of? Artificial fibers do not allow the skin to breathe. Rather they trap moisture, whether it's your baby's perspiration, urine, or any other moisture, leaving your baby hot and sweaty instead of cool and comfortable, even in weather that might not normally cause him to be hot and sweaty. One hundred percent natural fiber sheets (usually cotton) are a much better choice.

## Ⓔ *Essential*

If you feel that, despite the absence of flame retardant or because of the absence of it, 100 percent natural fiber sheets are best, be sure your baby's pajamas are made of 100 percent cotton as well. Again, both carcinogens and the nature of the fabric are an issue. Artificial material does not allow the perspiration to escape the way cotton does; in fact, the nature of the fabric is such that it promotes sweat.

## Get the Right Clothes for Sleeping

If you choose to have your baby sleep in 100 percent natural fiber pajamas on 100 percent natural fiber sheets, which haven't been treated to make them flame retardant, you'll need to be more careful than ever of fire precautions. Don't go into your baby's room or allow anyone else to so with a lit cigarette or pipe. Be wary of space heaters and other devices that are known hazards. Have good smoke detectors in the house, including one near the kitchen and one near your baby's room, so that in case of a fire incident you are warned or awakened, if you're sleeping. If you're taking all these precautions, you might consider whether it's more important to you to put your baby to sleep in flame-retardant pajamas on flame-retardant sheets or to have him in all-natural pajamas on all-natural sheets, neither of which is chemically treated. The choice is yours. Decide which choice you're more comfortable with.

## Other Suffocation Hazards

Your baby should not have a pillow in his crib until he is at least two years old. Babies do not need pillows, and there is a serious risk of suffocation associated with the use of pillows by children under age two. By the same token, you don't want to use too heavy a blanket on him either. A "blankie" is typically a thin, lightweight receiving blanket and is fine to use. A heavy blanket in a crib presents a suffocation hazard. While you don't want your baby to be cold, it's much better to raise the temperature in the house than to pile blankets on your baby or put one big heavy blanket on him. You can also dress him in two sleepers for warmth if need be.

Never allow a young baby to sleep on a sofa, bean-bag chair, featherbed, or any other surface that is not very firm. If he's old enough to roll over, he could wind up face-down in the soft surface and be smothered. In addition, on a sofa, even if he can't roll over yet, he can turn his head, get his face up against the soft back of the sofa, and be smothered against it.

This is even more true if you are napping with him and place him between you and the back of the sofa, thinking you're providing safety by keeping him from rolling off. In your sleep, you could roll toward him, wedge him more firmly against the back of the sofa, and help to smother him.

Even if the back of your sofa feels firm against your back, it's a hazard for your baby.

## Ⓔ *Alert!*

If you cosleep or keep your baby in your bed at night rather than in a crib (discussed further in Chapter 8), be sure your mattress is extremely firm and replace it if it isn't. Remove your pillows and make sure the sheet and blanket aren't pulled up over your baby's face.

## SIDS

The most serious problem of all, because it's fatal, is SIDS. Sudden Infant Death Syndrome, commonly known by the acronym of SIDS, has also been called "crib death" and refers to the unexpected and unexplained death of an apparently healthy baby, most commonly during sleep. Doctors now feel that many of these cases are traceable to the baby's accidental smothering. Children under two years of age should not be given pillows, and babies of any age should sleep on only the firmest of mattresses. Most important, babies should be put to sleep on their backs, not their stomachs. A national campaign to promote this sleeping position is known as "Back to Sleep." All these precautions aid in minimizing the opportunities for your baby to die from lack of oxygen.

Once your baby is old enough to roll over in his crib, he may turn onto his stomach during the night, but by then he is past the age at which he is at the greatest risk from SIDS. The danger is highest among infants who cannot pick up their heads or roll over and whose faces sink into soft mattresses or loose sheets.

But not all cases of SIDS are traceable to smothering in soft mattresses or loose sheets. Though scientists and doctors don't know all the causes of SIDS, it does seem that these sudden and inexplicable deaths are triggered by more than one cause, rather than one specific thing. There are certain facts we do know about babies who are more likely to die of SIDS:

- Boy babies are more likely to die of SIDS than are girls.
- Children of younger mothers are more at risk than children of older mothers.

- Bottle-fed babies are more likely to die of SIDS than are breast-fed babies.
- Low-birth-weight babies are more at risk than are babies of normal birth weight.
- SIDS seems to run in the family. If you had one child die of SIDS, your subsequent children are at higher risk.

None of these factors is a sure indicator of a problem, and in fact, many babies who die of SIDS don't match any of the factors in the previous list. Most babies who die of SIDS were apparently quite healthy up until the time of their death.

There does seem to be some correlation between babies who die of SIDS and mothers who smoke either during pregnancy or thereafter. If you smoke, quitting is a healthy move not only for yourself, but also for your baby. There has also been a connection made between over-heated babies and SIDS. SIDS is the leading cause of death in babies whose ages range between one month old and one year old.

## Ⓔ *Essential*

Few parents have bedrooms large enough to accommodate all their own furniture and all of their baby's things, too. A room of his own or at least a room he shares with an older sibling is all but a necessity for your child, if only as a place where his belongings . . . belong.

## Baby's Own Room

Even if your baby is sharing a family bed with you, you will probably want him to have his own room or to have a place in his older sibling's room. Even if he may not sleep there for several years, as he grows older it's good for him to know there's a place he can think of as his, where he can sleep when he gets older. On a more practical level, you'll need a place to put a chest of drawers or other piece of furniture in which to keep his clothes, a closet in which to keep clothes that hang, a toy chest or other suitable furniture in which to store toys, and perhaps other furniture and belongings as well.

What else should be in Baby's room besides his crib or bassinet? You may also want to set his room up as the safest play area in the house, perhaps setting his swing up in his room rather than in the living room, or situating his playpen there, or simply letting him play in his room when he's old enough to crawl around on the floor. He'll have toys that are meant for spreading out, pushing around with small hands, or otherwise best suited to floor play, and you may elect to have him do much of that in his room.

## Chapter 8

# The Family Bed

While many parents take their babies into bed with them only as a last resort when there's no other way to calm the crying child, a growing number of parents are reverting to an old and time-tested practice, known these days as "cosleeping" or "the family bed." There are assorted variations on this practice, but true cosleeping involves the child (and sometimes two or more children) sleeping all night in the bed with her parents. There is much to be said both for and against these methods.

## *Parents and Baby Sharing a Room*

This is a step short of true cosleeping: Many parents, though they aren't interested in a "family bed" arrangement, do put their baby's crib in the room with them, especially in the first few days after the baby is born.

**Fact**

> In some families, the baby sleeps in the family bed but naps in a crib. Parents who do this often do it for safety reasons. The parent who doesn't want to lie down every time Baby does may be concerned about leaving him alone in the family bed for his nap.

### Advantages

There are many good reasons parents want to have their baby close. They like being able to watch him and listen to him as he sleeps or as he plays in his crib. They feel more secure being in the same room with their baby. If he has any sort of problem, such as choking during the night, they are more likely to hear and be able to come to his aid instantaneously. While the baby still takes nighttime feedings, the parents are right there in the same room to scoop the baby out of his crib when he wakens. If he's bottle-feeding, one parent can hold the baby while the other goes off to get the bottle, or the parent who's holding the baby can carry him to the kitchen when he or she goes to get the bottle. If the baby is nursing, Mom can retrieve him from his crib and sit down in a chair or on the bed and quickly offer him her breast before he works up to a full-throated wail.

### Disadvantages

You may find that there are several disadvantages to having your baby's crib in your bedroom. When your baby wakes up during the night, resettles, and goes back to sleep, the slight sounds he makes are likely to awaken you and your spouse, even though your baby doesn't need attention. When you are getting ready for bed and when you get up in the morning, the sounds you make, from squeaking bedsprings as you settle down to the ringing of your alarm clock in the morning to the sound of the TV you may watch in bed at night to the conversations you have together may all awaken your baby. If your baby wakes up before you do in the morning and he's alone in his own room, he may play happily in his crib for a little while or just lie there contentedly. But if he sees you lying within his view, even though you're still asleep, he's more likely to start to fuss and demand attention. Last, but certainly not least, you and/or your spouse may feel more inhibited about love-making when your baby is in the same room.

## *Parents and Baby Sharing a Bed*

All of these negative aspects to having your baby's crib in the room also apply to cosleeping, but parents who opt to cosleep usually do so for stronger reasons than just convenience. They truly enjoy having their baby next to or between them, and for them, the advantages of having Baby in their bed far outweigh the additional, serious disadvantages.

What are the advantages of having your baby in your bed? To begin with, babies are soothed by the touch of their parents at any time, day or night, awake or asleep. The child who sleeps secure in the warmth and close touch of her mom and/or her dad is a child who is drawing a strong sense of security and well-being from the actual physical contact.

If the baby wakes during the night with the sniffles, you'll wake up and hear her quickly. Even the quietest sniffle, if it recurs, will wake you and get your attention. If the baby spits up, you'll know that, too. You won't unknowingly leave her lying all night in a crib that she's spit up into, with regurgitated milk that's now going sour.

If the room is too warm or too cold, you'll be aware of it, since you're in the same room and under the same covers as Baby is. If your baby wakes from a bad dream, Mom and Dad are right there beside him. He may not scream or cry or even whimper. Feeling or seeing, if there is a nightlight, the familiar forms of his parents beside him, he will very possibly feel secure enough to close his eyes and work his way back to sleep, without the terror he might have felt otherwise and without waking you up.

More seriously, if your baby starts to choke, you'll hear her right away and be able to help her. Should she stop breathing, be it from sleep apnea, from SIDS, or from some other cause, you may realize it, wake up with a start, and be able to take measures to try to get her breathing again right away.

## Cosleeping and Nursing

Perhaps the greatest beneficiaries of a family bed sleeping arrangement are the nursing baby and her mom. When your baby wakes up beside you during the night and is hungry or just wants to suckle a little for the relaxation she needs to help herself back to sleep, she can latch on to a nipple and begin to feed. Some mothers under these circumstances don't even wake up or awaken just barely, take note of the fact that the baby is feeding, and go back to sleep. It's so much less disturbing to your sleep than having to get up, retrieve the baby from the crib (even if her crib is in your room), sit down somewhere (whether it's your bed or a chair or the living room sofa) to hold the baby and nurse her, then get up, return her to her crib, and return to your bed, by which time you're fully wide-awake and may lie in bed quite a while before you can get back to sleep.

## Ⓔ *Alert!*

Breastfeeding an infant who is cosleeping should be done with the utmost of caution. The Consumer Product Safety Commission (CPSC) says that mothers who breast-feed should be alerted to the hazard of smothering their baby and should be encouraged to return the baby to the crib after breastfeeding.

Your baby won't wake up as fully either. She doesn't have to work her way up to a full-throated cry to get your attention if she's hungry. She'll learn quickly that she can just turn her head and find your breast and then suckle on it until she's had her fill. Since she hasn't awakened as fully, she has a much better chance of getting back to sleep easily. So that's three of you who can sleep better: the baby, you, and your spouse. Remember that babies who breastfeed need to feed more often; so if you're nursing your child, you can expect more frequent awakenings, at least in the early months. It is a great convenience to have her right there in bed with you when she's hungry.

If you're feeding your baby infant formula, you can still have some of the ease of breastfeeding if you cosleep. You can keep the formula by the side of the bed and simply reach for it when she wakes to feed.

## *Disadvantages of Cosleeping*

It should be strongly emphasized, however, that cosleeping has its serious disadvantages. Besides the more obvious inconveniences already covered in the discussion of cribs, there are other important considerations to take into account when you make your decision.

### Warnings from the AAP and CPSC

Both the American Academy of Pediatrics (AAP) and the CPSC have taken stands against cosleeping. The AAP has published cautionary warnings about infants being smothered under bedclothes or the weight of a much heavier adult. The CPSC issued a warning against placing babies in adult beds, citing a study which revealed that an average of sixty-four babies a year die from suffocation and strangulation from such a practice. Based on data for a seven-year period, the CPSC linked adult beds to at least 515 baby deaths with four major hazard patterns:

- Suffocation associated with cosleeping of adult and baby.
- Suffocation of an infant trapped or wedged between mattress and another object.
- Suffocation of an infant facedown on a waterbed mattress.
- Strangulation in rails or bed openings by entrapping the baby's head.

### Other Disadvantages

If your baby wakes during the night and doesn't cry, she might still wake you up despite her silence. If she's in her own crib and especially if that crib is in her own room, you won't know it if she awakens briefly but lies contentedly until she falls asleep again. But when she's in your bed and you're attuned to her as she lies there beside you, you're likely to awaken when she does, even if she utters only a gurgle. Conversely, the baby may wake up every time you or your spouse get up to use the bathroom, have a drink of water, or check on that noise you just heard.

But even if you are successful and Baby remains asleep on the bed, that's not the end of your concerns. You still need to give some thought to the possibility of her rolling over and falling out of bed or, if she's old enough to crawl, of her waking up and deliberately leaving the bed and wandering off. Some of the measures discussed in the safety section that follows will help, but they're not ironclad prevention against an accident.

If she's a very light sleeper, she might wake up every time one of you rolls over and resettles. If she's that light a sleeper, she might truly do better in her own crib and not in a family bed. If yours is a household in which the phone often rings late at night or early in the morning and you keep a phone in your bedroom, the baby's sleep is exceedingly likely to be disturbed by the ringing.

### ⓔ *Essential*

You'll know when your baby moves from REM sleep to non-REM sleep. Her eyes will stop moving, her body parts will stop moving and twitching, and at that point you should be able to escape without her waking up and realizing you've decamped for the kitchen or the living room.

Another problem is that if the baby is used to having you next to her when she sleeps, she's likely to be unable to fall asleep unless at least one of you is lying beside her. You may need to stretch out on the bed next to your baby every night and stay there at least until she is in her first deep sleep—which is likely to be half an hour for a baby under six months old, though within ten minutes or so for a baby older than that.

If your baby wets the bed, it's your bed, and the sheets you have to change are much larger and more cumbersome than changing a crib sheet. Changing the sheets on a double bed, queen-size bed, or king-size bed can be a major production compared to changing a crib sheet. Three people's sleep (or more, if you have another child sleeping in with you) will have to be disturbed so you can change the sheets.

## Cosleeping and Safety

If you choose to cosleep, you are under an obligation to make the experience as safe for your baby as possible. The CPSC has said of infant mortalities associated with adult beds that, "One of the most tragic aspects of these deaths is that they are largely preventable." Their recommendations are not cosleeping at all or putting an infant to sleep in an adult bed. If you are determined to cosleep, safety must come first.

### Beds

The same safety measures and standards that apply to cribs should be used in regard to your bed. First, be sure that your mattress is ultrafirm; if possible, buy a new one. Under no circumstances should a baby sleep on a waterbed. Not only is there a risk of his smothering in the giving mattress, but he also can get wedged between the water mattress and the bed's frame. The rule that a baby should always be put to sleep on his back still applies.

### Size Matters

If you're going to have a family bed, make it a king-size one if you have that option. Your bedroom may not be large enough, or you may not have the budget for a whole new bed (though a firm new mattress is important). But if it's at all possible, get a king-size bed, and not only will your baby have farther to roll before getting out of bed, but you and your spouse will also have more room to get comfortable in—especially when Baby decides she wants to lie horizontally between you. Otherwise you may be the one falling off the edge. Keep in mind that your baby will need more room as she grows.

According to the AAP, the argument that in cultures where cosleeping is prevalent that babies suffer no ill-effects is misleading. The organization points out that in these cultures, families almost never sleep on soft mattresses with bulky covers.

Another hazard that needs to be considered before opting for a family bed is the weight of both parents. Obese parents are not good candidates for cosleeping since they may not be as aware of the extent to which their girth extends over Baby. An obese mom or dad who is lying snuggled next to Baby and rolls over toward him is jeopardizing him greatly.

Some parents try to solve the dilemma of keeping their baby in the bed by putting one side of the bed up against the wall. At first thought, this seems an eminently sensible thing to do—it would be hard for Baby to roll off that way. But in fact, it's a very bad idea, as your baby can easily become trapped in the small space between the mattress and the wall and can even suffocate. The CPSC reports that between January 1970 and December 1997, twenty babies died just that way.

A good alternative plan is to place your bed as close to the floor as possible. Eliminate the frame; eliminate the box spring as well, if you're willing. With the mattress much closer to the floor, even if Baby rolls out of the bed, he hasn't far to fall. A blanket spread out next to the mattress on the floor will help cushion his fall even further.

## Ⓔ *Alert!*

If any member of the family is allergic to dust, be aware that dust is more prevalent down on the floor. By lowering the mattress to just above the floor, you expose that family member to a greater intake of allergy-inducing dust. In this case, be scrupulous about vacuuming the floor often and being extra careful about cleanliness in general and dusting and vacuuming in particular.

While we're talking about eliminating things for safety, how about eliminating your headboard and footboard? They present hazards, too. Your baby can get an arm or leg or her head trapped between any slats or other apertures in your headboard or footboard. Just as the baby's crib slats should be close together, so too should the space between your headboard or footboard slats be narrow enough that there's no chance of Baby's head fitting between them and getting wedged. Other hazards include peeling paint from an old headboard or footboard and wrought iron head-boards and footboards, which are harder on Baby's head if she bangs up against them. (Again, there may be a peel-ing-paint hazard as well.) So if you do have a headboard and/or footboard on your bed, remove them if possible. At minimum, examine them for safety hazards.

## Ⓔ Essential

Always have an adult positioned between a baby and an older sibling, if you all share a bed. Though the older sibling will surely be much smaller and weigh much less than either you or your spouse, he will also be much less aware, and so the baby is at greater risk from him rolling over on her than she is from either you or your spouse doing so.

### Betwixt and Between?

Should your cosleeping baby sleep between the two of you or on the outside of one of you? Clearly the baby sleeping between you has little chance of rolling out of bed during the night. But he has two parents who need to be wary of rolling over onto him. If he sleeps between you and the edge, only one parent has to be careful not to roll onto him, and only one of you needs to sleep aware of the hazard. On the other hand, he's in more jeopardy of rolling off the bed. If he hasn't rolled over yet, he will one day soon enough. You know how sound a sleeper you are and your spouse is. You need to make the final decision as to whether your baby is safer between you and your spouse or on the outside of one of you.

### Bed Coverings and Pillows

If you must sleep on a pillow, please keep your baby's face far away from it. Preferably, don't use a pillow in a family bed until the baby is at least two years old. Keep the room warm enough so that you need only a light blanket. No heavy blankets, quilts, or anything else that might smother your baby if he gets under the covers.

When you get up in the morning, if you manage to exit the bed without awakening your baby, he'll be unprotected. It's best to stay in bed until he wakes up, but if that's simply not possible, you need a baby monitor with which you can listen for sounds indicating he has woken up. While you're starting your morning routine, your baby might be rolling out of bed. If he's already crawling, he might be liberating himself from the confines of the bed and examining his surroundings and getting into potentially harmful situations. If you absolutely must leave Baby alone in the bed, you need a baby monitor, a guard gate, and the precaution of removing all sharp, poisonous, or otherwise dangerous objects from his reach. Check on him often.

## The Sidecar Solution

Just as motorcycles can be fitted with sidecars for passengers, beds can be fitted with a type of sidecar for cosleepers. In fact, these devices sometimes are called "cosleepers." They're an ideal solution when parents want to let Baby sleep with them yet they are fearful of rolling over on him or of his falling out of the bed. If you just don't trust yourself; if you or your spouse regularly take prescription medications that make you groggy; if you have a double bed and no room for a king-size bed; if you have one child in your bed already and no room for a king-size bed; if you have dust allergies and sleeping close to the floor is impractical for you; or if for any other reason you're concerned about letting your baby sleep in your bed, a sidecar may be the ideal solution.

## Alert!

Never cosleep when you are under any alcoholic or pharmacologic influence that might make you groggy or alter your responses. This applies not only to drinking alcohol, but also to taking any prescription drugs that might affect your sleep or your response time. If you are under any sort of chemical influence, sleep apart from the baby, whether that means a night on the living room couch or putting Baby in a crib for one night.

What's a sidecar? A sidecar is a modified three-sided crib, whose height is adjusted to match the height of your bed, whose mattress lies firmly flush to the mattress of your larger bed, which has bars on three sides, keeping Baby in. In fact, some particularly handy parents modify regular cribs to turn them into sidecars. But if you're not Mr. or Ms. Fixit, you can buy a sidecar or cosleeper and attach it to your bed.

One other solution is a device called a "snuggle nest," which sits on your bed, holds your baby, and protects him from accidental rollovers or inadvertent escapes.

## *Privacy Aspects for Parents*

"But how do we make love if the baby is in the bed with us?" That's your question, isn't it? It's the question your friends will all ask of you, too. How do you manage to have any of the intimacy a couple certainly needs? The answer is simple: You don't "go to bed together" in bed!

What are your options?

- Leave the baby with a babysitter or a family member.
- Keep a baby monitor with you after baby has fallen asleep.
- Using a sheet or blanket, opt for the floor.
- Put the baby in a playpen.
- Find a fellow cosleeper among your friends and very frankly suggest trading an hour or two of time to watch each other's baby so each couple can have some time alone.

There are ways around the problem. It just requires a little creativity. Isn't lovemaking a creative act unto itself? So be creative about where and when as well as about how!

## Moving Baby Out of Your Bed

Some children leave the family bed of their own accord; others leave because their parents feel it's time. Some leave because a new sibling is on the way or has just been born. Some children make the transition as early as eighteen months of their own accord; others don't decide to leave until adolescence. Most kids who move out of the family bed on their own pick an age somewhere in between—perhaps between four and eight. Of course, children who leave at their parents' suggestion may be leaving at almost any age, depending on the reason. Is it because the child is too big, wiggles too much, takes up too much of the bed, and interferes with your sleep? Is it because of another pregnancy? Is it because either you or your spouse is simply no longer enjoying the cosleeping arrangement? Is it because of some change in the physical layout of your house, perhaps a new house with a smaller bedroom that cannot accommodate your king-size bed?

As a transition, your child may want to sleep on a separate mattress on the floor of your room. This is especially a good solution for the toddler who isn't quite ready to fully separate, though even older kids may want this arrangement for a while. If you're ending a cosleeping arrangement because of a new baby, it's best to ease the first child out of the family bed a few weeks before the new sibling is expected.

If moving the child out is your idea, ways to tempt him include suggesting that he's such a big boy that maybe he wants to sleep in a big-boy bed in his own room; offering him theme-decorated sheets or a special bed such as a canopied bed or one shaped like a race car; or offering him a gift unrelated to the actual sleeping arrangements but offered as a gift or privilege "now that you're old enough to sleep in your own bed." The child may want his own bed for privacy reasons. He may want his own bed even though you're not particularly eager to see him go. But if he is ready, let him go. The bed may feel empty for a time. But leaving the family bed is part of growing up. Sooner or later, whether it's at your behest or on his own, it's going to happen.

## Chapter 9

# Adjusting to New Surroundings

Even the best of sleepers can be thrown off track by a change in sleeping quarters. In new surroundings, your baby may suddenly resist going to sleep, wake several times, and have great difficulty falling asleep again. What are the circumstances that can result in your baby's finding herself in new surroundings? Certainly a vacation is one such cause, and another is a short stay at Grandma's, or even a change within your own home from one room to another, and, yes, even Daylight Savings Time!

## *Changes at Home*

A "change" of location for your baby can occur right within your own home. If the change is a minimal one, such as moving his crib from one room to another in the same house, you may think the impact on him will be little if any. But understand that from his vantage point on the mattress of the crib, though the crib may be familiar, the whole world outside it is not. The furniture is different. Even if it is the same, it's arranged differently so it appears different to him. The color of paint or pattern of wallpaper on the other side of the bars, the color of the carpet, and the pattern of shadows on the wall at night, whether from a hall light, a streetlight, a night-light, or other source is different than it was in his previous room. Even the sounds may be different in this room than in his old one. All this adds up to unfamiliarity, and unfamiliarity is disturbing at his age.

## Ⓔ *Essential*

> Your baby is likely to fear abandonment, too, in a big move. Since everything else has changed—his familiar room has "gone away"—he fears that you may have gone away, too.

### Moving to a New Home

What if your home itself changes? Often a young family, starting to grow, will find a move to a larger house necessary. The move may be precipitated by a new pregnancy, by needing more room for your existing family, or it may simply be a matter of the family being now able to afford a larger house or being able to move to a house from an apartment. The move may not have anything to do with family size or family purchasing power at all; maybe you are moving to another city or town or simply relocating within your city or town to live in another neighborhood. No matter the reason, the result is that your baby is going to find herself in different surroundings.

## Departing from the Crib

Most parents (except cosleepers) keep their babies in cribs until around age two, or toilet training, or until the baby is able to climb out on his own, at which point it's safer to put him into a bed. But sometimes it's necessary to move the baby to a bed sooner, perhaps because Mom is pregnant again and will need the crib for the new baby. You'll want to make the switch before the new baby is due, not only so your toddler doesn't have too many changes to get used to at once, but also in case the new baby arrives unexpectedly early.

You can make a big deal out of the new bed and even have a "graduation party" if you wish. If your toddler is resistant to the idea of giving up his crib, you can tempt him with new sheets with his favorite cartoon characters on them or some other treat that will make the new bed more attractive. You can even point out that the dog or cat can now sleep on the bed with him, and won't that be nice?

The transition will be easier if the toddler is himself a second child; he'll be eager to emulate his older sibling, who's a big boy or big girl sleeping on a big-boy bed or big-girl bed, as your toddler is now about to do. If there's no older sibling to point to, then "just like Mommy and Daddy" can be your catch phrase.

### Alert!

If your toddler is a bit young for a real bed, consider giving him just a mattress on the floor at first or getting a protective guard rail to keep him from rolling out. If you don't choose either of these options, at least put some pillows on the floor so that if he does roll out he lands softly.

### Making the New Seem Old

The key to a successful transition is to try to make the new room as familiar as possible. If it's practical, it may help to put the new bed in the same place the crib was. This way, the room will look familiar when your toddler wakes up during the night to resettle himself. If you're putting an expected new baby in the same room with the toddler you're moving out of the crib, move the crib to another spot in the room and put the toddler's new bed in the spot where his crib was. You might even want to take the crib down for a month or two and then put it back together before the new baby is born.

In the case of a move from one house to another, you might consider painting the walls of his room the same color as the walls of his room in the house you're moving from. That way, when he looks out between the bars of his crib on the wall side, he sees the same color as always.

In addition, to whatever extent it's practical, you can try to arrange his furniture in a manner similar to its arrangement in his first room. When he looks out the bars of the crib on the other side, he'll still see the familiar toy chest in its usual place, the corner of the dresser, and so on.

If he's used to having a night-light or to having some light coming into the room from a hallway light, try to emulate the same level of light he's used to. If he's used to sleeping in the dark but seems fearful after the move or during the temporary stay in unfamiliar quarters, you can try leaving a night-light on for him. Though it will emphasize the unfamiliarity of the room, he will be able to see that there is nothing fearful. The light will illuminate Mr. Bear or whatever other stuffed furry friends he has in the crib with him, whose presence will reassure him.

## ⓔ *Essential*

If he's used to hearing music or the sound of the TV coming from the living room, maintaining these familiar sounds can aid in reassuring him, too. The more familiarity you can lend to his new or temporary surroundings, the more security you can offer him. Even familiar smells can help, if this is something you can arrange.

## Moving Baby to Her Own Room

Sometimes the change in your baby's surroundings is a much simpler one: moving her into her own room. You've had her crib in your room because you wanted to have her nearby. You wanted to have her where you could check on her during the night, but she's reached an age at which you're comfortable that she doesn't have any health issues, and all is well. You've had her crib in your room because it was handier for middle-of-the-night feedings, but now she's sleeping through the night. You want to be able to make love again without concern that the baby is in your room. You want to turn the 11:00 P.M. news on in the bedroom and turn the volume up to a comfortable level without worrying that you'll wake the baby.

## Ⓔ *Alert!*

If you are moving her out of her crib at the same time you're moving her out of her room, you can still pile her crib toys on the new bed. Emphasize that she's a "big girl" now and she can have her own room and a "big-girl bed!" But don't be surprised if she's less enthusiastic than you are about this change.

The room she's moving into may be hers alone or one she's sharing with a sibling. If there's an older brother or sister in the room, he may wake her or keep her from falling asleep in the first place, if he's noisy or keeps a bright light on. He may even do it "by accident on purpose," if he's at all resentful of having to share a room that was formerly his exclusively. On the other hand, the baby may find it easier to fall asleep with someone in the room, if she's used to having you in the room with her. However, if she's a little older, she may be intrigued by what her older sibling is doing and want to stay up and be part of the activity.

Depending on the baby's age, the switch from your room to her own room may be concurrent with the change from a crib to a "big-girl bed," but other than that, it's better not to make too many changes at once. Keep her crib toys the same, and keep the same blanket in the crib or new bed. (Even if she now has a proper tucked-in blanket to lie under, she may want to use her old crib blanket as a "blankie" or security blanket.) Give her the security of as many familiar things as you can offer her in her new surroundings.

When you move her into her own room, be sure to give her a night-light, at least for the first few nights, so that if she wakes up and knows she's somewhere unaccustomed, she can at least see that she's in a room of the same familiar house. If you're moving her from a crib to a bed, be sure there's a night-light to provide her adequate light in case she gets out of bed or falls out of bed.

Check the new room before you move her in there, looking for any possible fear source: eerie shadows cast by tree limbs outside, scary-shaped stains on the ceiling, or other sights or sounds that might cause concern to a little one. Eliminate or mask any sight or sound you identify as something that might possibly induce fear in the baby.

## Changes When Traveling

Whether you take to the road in a recreational vehicle, stay in a Paris hotel or a cabin in the woods, or leave Baby for a night or weekend at Grandma's, it's not the familiar room she's used to, and she probably won't be in her same familiar crib, either. The baby who's been "good as gold" at night and who's been such a joy when she visits at Grandma's during the day might suddenly turn into a little monster who keeps you (or Grandma) up half the night with her crying.

### Making New Surroundings More Comfortable

Again, one way to help your baby adjust to the new surroundings is by making them seem as familiar as possible. Clearly you can't transport to Grandma's or to the hotel the toy chest or dresser he sees when he looks out the bars of his crib at home. But whether you're leaving him at Grandma's or taking him on vacation, bring some or all of his crib toys (depending on how many he has). The familiarity of Mr. Bear or Fluffy Rabbit or whoever inhabits his little world, perched in his new or temporary crib, will help make the new surroundings seem more familiar.

The more you can reassure him that there is nothing fearful out there, the better. If you can show him something familiar in his surroundings, you'll be even better off.

### The Hotel Crib

The best defense when it comes to your baby's sleeping arrangements when you travel is a good offense. Call the hotel and reserve a crib. Make sure they understand that a crib must be put aside for you. When you arrive, ask for the crib immediately. Inspect it and look for the same things you would if you were buying a crib for the house. Hotel cribs tend to get a good workout. Check to see that it is stable. Test to make sure it won't collapse when your baby moves around. Are there any sharp points or edges? Is there any peeling paint? Is there a good, firm mattress and no soft pillows or bumpers?

## Ⓔ *Question?*

**Should I let my baby sleep between me and my spouse and risk getting him used to sleeping with us?**
Most family bed advocates don't recommend the child sleeping between the parents. You establish a bad precedent. You're probably better off letting him sleep on a bed or mattress by himself.

### When There's No Crib

Despite your best efforts, occasionally you'll find yourself in a situation in which there's no crib for your baby to sleep in while you're on vacation or otherwise away from home. What can you do in such a predicament?

Plan ahead. The first choice is to buy a portable crib or a "pack-and-play" crib or playpen, using the same criteria for choosing as you would a traditional crib. Also stay current on manufacturers' recalls. For this information, contact the U.S. Consumer Product Safety Commission hotline at ✆(800) 638-2772, or at ✍*www.cpsc.gov.*

If your baby is still young enough to fit comfortably in a carrier and isn't rolling over yet, he may be happy to sleep through the night there. Strapped in, he's secure. The carrier is familiar to him. Problem solved!

Failing all the previously mentioned suggestions, if he's somewhat older, you might not have any other choice but to place a mattress on the floor and let him sleep there. Should he roll out of bed during the night, he won't have far to fall. The hazard that remains is that he can walk or crawl away and might fall down the stairs, open the front door, get into something dangerous in one of the rooms, or otherwise get into trouble. Just what he can get into will depend, of course, both on how old he is and on what opportunities present themselves in these surroundings. The hazards are different for a four-month-old and a fourteen-month-old.

If for some reason you aren't able to put him to bed on a mattress on the floor, your remaining option is to let him sleep in a real bed and put pillows alongside the bed on the floor. This way, should he fall out, he will fall to the soft surface of a pillow. However, note that this is not safe for a newborn or younger infant.

### Time Zone Shifts

Another disruptive factor that can interfere with your baby's sleep schedule is a time zone shift. If you've flown from the East Coast to the West Coast, suddenly there's a three-hour difference in time to which you and baby must adjust. If you're visiting for just three or four days, it doesn't pay to try to get your baby in sync with the new time zone. Keep her as close to her home schedule as possible, despite the difference in time. This will be easier if you've only gone one time zone away than if you've gone two or three or farther.

But if you're visiting for ten days or two weeks and particularly if it's only a one-time-zone shift, it will be easier if you can get your baby onto the local time. If you're not visiting but have moved from one time zone to another, of course it's necessary. You do this in the same way that you regulate her in the switch from Daylight Savings Time to Standard Time or vice versa: in short increments. Under the circumstances, though, ten-minute increments won't effect the change you need quickly enough. Try putting her to bed twenty minutes earlier or later each day, and to be synchronized with your hosts as easily as possible, you might want to try adjusting the baby's schedule before you leave, so that she's already on your hosts' local time when you get to your destination.

## Ⓔ *Alert!*

If the baby is not used to sleeping in your room, then suddenly sharing a room with you can have a couple of downsides. First, the noise you make, no matter how quiet you are, may wake her up if you're sharing a room. Second, she may get accustomed to it and insist on your presence at home.

### Familiar Routines

If the baby isn't used to sleeping in the same room with you, it's preferable to keep her in a separate room when you're on vacation. Of course, this may not be possible. If you're staying in a hotel, you can't put her in a separate hotel room (though two different rooms of a suite would be workable). If you're staying with relatives, they may not have two guest rooms available. The baby may have to sleep in your room or in the same room as her cousin.

But try to keep things as similar to the way they are at home as possible. Try to retain your usual routine. If you normally feed, then bathe your baby, and then put him to bed at 6:30 P.M., try to follow the same routine now. If you usually give him a massage, sing him a song, and say a prayer, do the same thing now. Don't be inhibited by the presence of others, and try not to be persuaded when someone says, "You're on vacation. You don't have to stick to your usual routine." No, you don't have to, but it will make things go a lot more smoothly for your baby.

Again, if you have his usual crib toys, his favorite "blankie," and anything else that feels like "home" to him, it will help.

## Visiting Relatives in Their Home

Sometimes family vacations involve traveling to visit relatives and stay at their house. Under these circumstances, you and your baby are going to have to live by the schedules of your relatives, and there will be other changes for your baby to get used to as well.

### Handling New Noise

You can hardly ask your hosts to be quiet all evening. You aren't quiet all evening in your house. But the sounds in the host's home may be louder or simply different. Perhaps you:

- Visit relatives whose living room is nearer to the baby's room, and the sound of voices and of the TV or stereo carries more loudly to her room.
- Visit a home where one family member is hard of hearing and keeps the TV, radio, or stereo extra loud.
- Visit a home where there's a noisy young child, and your baby is not used to having an active three-year-old screeching around the house.
- Experience much more street noise in the home you're visiting than your baby is used to in your own house.
- Visit relatives who live in an apartment and have noisy neighbors.

You have little control over these things. But if you're prepared, you can bring or find a device that will create a white sound to help block out some of the noise.

## Scheduling Different Meal Times

Let's say you're used to feeding your baby her cereal or pureed carrots at the dinner table, with the two of you, at 6:30 P.M. every evening and then putting her to bed at 7:30 P.M. Suddenly you're at your sister's house, where dinner isn't served until 7:00 P.M. What are your options? You can:

- Feed your baby ahead of the family dinner and get her to bed on time.

- Feed her at 7:00 P.M. with everyone else and then put her right to bed on a full stomach.
- Feed her at 7:00 P.M. with the others and not put her to bed until 8:00 or 8:30 P.M.
- Ask your sister whether she can change her family's dinner hour for the duration of your visit to accommodate your baby's schedule.

Obviously, the best solution is the one that disrupts your baby's schedule as little as possible—which would be the first option. Failing that, other solutions would depend on how comfortable you are asking your sister for favors, how flexible your sister is, and how feasible the schedule change is for the others in her family.

 **Fact**

You may find that the changes you institute in your baby's schedule while on vacation work better for you even at home. But if not, get him back on track on his regular schedule as soon as you return home.

### Scheduling Different Naptimes

But what if your brother-in-law, being a jovial and genial host, insists on taking you out to dinner several of the days you're there? What if your host is not used to cooking for large groups and is daunted by the prospect of cooking for so many people and insists that you're all going to eat out while you're there visiting? What if there are no reliable babysitters available or you don't have the money in the budget for hiring a sitter?

Now not only are you dealing with a family dinner hour that might be later than what you're accustomed to, but you're also dealing with eating in a restaurant, which is never as quick as eating at home. Nor can you get up and put the baby to bed in the middle of your dinner, as you would be able to do at home. What to do?

You're going to have to put the baby to bed late. You're certainly within your rights to politely request that you eat as early as is comfortable for your hosts to avoid getting your baby any further off schedule than is necessary. But accept the fact that there's going to be some schedule shifting. You're going to find yourself still sitting at the dinner table in the restaurant at ten minutes of eight, holding a fussy, sleepy baby or one who has gone to sleep on your shoulder, whose bedtime was almost two hours ago.

### Special Problems for Cosleepers

If your family members are cosleepers and the mattress on the guest bed where you're vacationing is soft, you have yet another problem. A soft mattress is a hazard for your baby. Yet you can hardly demand that your hosts buy a new mattress for their bed. In a hotel, you can request the room with the firmest mattress that's available, but even that is no guarantee. If you can bring with you a portable crib that has a good, firm mattress, it would be worth the extra hassle to be sure your baby has a safe mattress to sleep on. And, though your baby will not be spending the night in bed with you, it's certainly the better of the two options. Perhaps you can put him to sleep on the hotel bed with you, then transfer him to the crib after he is soundly asleep.

Another potential problem for cosleepers is that the family members you're visiting may not approve. By exposing your sleeping arrangement to them, you are letting yourself in for a lot of negative commentary. There's no easy solution. Be prepared to meet their objections with persuasive arguments of your own, or prepare them in advance by telling them that the baby sleeps in with you and that you don't need a portable crib, thank you very much.

 **Alert!**

Naps in the car do not affect a young infant who has not yet consolidated her sleep. The warning about disrupting sleep patterns only applies to older babies who sleep for long stretches at once.

## Sleeping in the Car

It's a simple fact: Put the average baby in a car and, unless she's recently awakened from a nap, she's likely to fall asleep in just a short distance. Are you traveling by car on your vacation? Count on the motion of the car to put your baby to sleep.

Having her sleep in the car is certainly far better than having her cry or become restless in the car, but it does have its downside, notably the fact that if she sleeps for any meaningful period it may interfere with her sched-uled nap or bedtime.

One way to cope is to set out on your trip just before she's due for a nap. Does she still nap in the morning? Instead of starting your journey at 7:00 or 8:00 A.M., wait until 10:00 A.M. (or whatever time you'd normally put her in for her nap) to actually get on the road. Then settle her in the car in her car seat and go. Your baby will fall asleep in the car rather quickly and probably nap for around the length of time she usually does. If you arrive at your desti-nation before she awakens, try to remove the car seat with-out waking the baby. If she awakens before you arrive, try to keep her awake until she's due for her next nap. Then, if you're still on the road, let the motion of the car lull her to sleep again. If she naps at approximately her usual time for approximately the usual length of nap, she should be ready for her bedtime right on schedule.

If your road trip is a long one and your baby falls asleep for the night before you arrive at your destination or at an interim destination, such as a motel where you will spend the night, you now have the question of what to do: wake her up and put her to bed or try to get her to bed without awakening her.

Some babies and older children, too, will not be upset if they wake up in the middle of the night in a strange place. But others will be very upset if they wake up in the middle of the night in a strange place with no memory of how they got there. This will then make it harder to get them back to sleep. Which type is your baby? If she's the type who won't be upset should she awaken during the night in a strange place, by all means try to get her out of the car and into the house or motel without waking her. But if she's the type who will get upset should she awaken in a strange place in the middle of the night and be confused, then you're better off waking her up and letting her see where she is before putting her back to bed once you get her inside.

## Ⓔ *Essential*

If you do wake your baby up and then put her back to bed in the house or motel, go through an abbreviated version of her usual bedtime routine. You may not want to take the time to bathe her, which might make her more wide-awake. You don't need to do everything you normally do. But give her at least a brief version of what she's used to at home. The familiarity will help soothe her into relaxing in her present surroundings.

Waking her up and putting her back to bed will also give you a chance to change her diaper and get her into her nightclothes (and out of any outerwear she may be wearing, such as a jacket).

## Day Care

A parent whose child is in day care is presented with a host of additional considerations and decisions. A choice of facility may be as easy as the service provided in-house by your company or as difficult as trying to decide among a dozen or more caregivers ranging from a mom working out of her home to a large chain operation. The answer is highly personal to you and your needs. You should question and investigate each candidate fully and completely before you entrust your baby to a third party.

As far as sleeping and daily routine goes, get a full rundown of the caregiver's schedule and see how it fits into your philosophy and goals. The time of arrival and pickup is crucial, not only to your baby's needs, but also to yours. How much time do you want to spend with your baby? If you pick up your baby after work, is there sufficient time in the evening for some quality time? If not, will you consider shifting your wakeup schedule and that of your baby to early morning so that you can spend an hour or two together before the workday begins?

## Ⓔ *Fact*

Company-operated day care centers have proven very popular and a good investment for management. Parents are allowed time to visit their children during the day, which increases morale and company loyalty. If your company does not offer day care, consider requesting it.

Don't fight a day care center's schedule or routine. Work with it and fit it into yours. It is the only practical thing to do. Any good day care center operates on sound principles and follows accepted childrearing techniques. That means that an appropriate sleep routine should be employed as a matter of course. If your day care center's routine differs significantly from what you know and believe is right for your child, find a different one.

If your child is old enough to realize she is being left with someone other than you, she may initially react to the separation in ways that disrupt sleep. Separation anxiety may cause sleeplessness, night terrors, and nightmares. Use the methods already discussed to cope with these problems, and the problems should subside quickly.

## Ⓔ *Essential*

Babies react to illness differently. Some are demanding, and some just want to be left in peace. Regardless of how your baby appears, your job is to watch him closely and carefully, note any changes in his symptoms (to relay to his doctor), keep him as comfortable as possible, and nurse him back to health.

### Sickness and Health

There is nothing so emotionally and physically draining or disruptive to the household routine as a sick infant. Your instinct will be to put everything on hold while you watch over and nurse your sick baby. Your instinct is correct. Depending on your baby's level of illness and guided by your pediatrician, your daily routine will be altered, and the rules will be broken. You can get back to normal when your baby is well again.

### Running the Household

An infant with a slight cold will require less of a wrenching household makeover than one with bronchitis or chronic illness. Each member of your household will be affected in some way. Adults will either have to lead, follow, or get out of the way. Other children must understand that they are not being mistreated or ignored, but reminded that "every member of our family must be taken care of properly when we are sick, and we need your help in this."

### The Sleep Routine

The sleep routine is probably shot. Sick infants will disrupt the sleep routine on many fronts. Coughing, stuffy noses, and sneezing keep them and you awake. Fever may keep them listless and sleeping at odd hours. You can only do the best you can do in trying to maintain the old cycles, but don't fret if it's not possible. Do whatever it takes to keep your child comfortable. If the baby sleeps better in her carriage, forget the crib. If you want to hold her in your bed, do it. If your bedmate complains, there's always the couch or guest room. For a few days, Baby comes first.

## Ⓔ *Alert!*

Rest is the most important ingredient in a sick baby's recuperation. But be alert to the fact that excessive sleep may indicate a more serious condition. If your baby naps much more than the three hours he normally does, contact your pediatrician.

### Medications

No too long ago, doctors were freely prescribing all kinds of medications in the belief that modern pharmaceuticals could do no wrong—painkillers, antihistamines, tranquilizers, and sedatives. That thinking has changed. Doctors are now careful to take advantage of today's miracle drugs without indiscriminate dosing. Some medications may cause sleep disruptions. Your pediatrician is well versed in drug reactions and side effects and will answer any questions you might have as to prescribing or withholding any medication for your baby.

There are some who believe that nature should take its course—let a fever burn out, let the body's defense mechanisms do their thing, feed a cold, starve a fever, etc. That is not informed thinking. A fever may be a killer, not a healer. Lack of proper nourishment may hinder healing, not help it. That is up to your doctor to decide. If you are unhappy with your pediatrician's advice, seek a second opinion. If they both agree, rethink your objections.

## *Honor His Fears—Within Reason*

Whether the change in your baby's sleeping circumstances is permanent (as in the case of a move from one house to another or from one room to another) or is temporary (as in the case of a vacation or a night spent at Grandma's), he is likely to be fearful at first. Honor his fears to a point. Don't let your baby use the change as an excuse to get used to being up late or sleeping in your bed (if you don't have a family bed).

You may need to stay with him while he falls asleep, even if you don't usually do that. You may need to hold him or rock him, things you might not normally do. You may need to make some other type of accommodation. But if the change in his sleeping circumstances is permanent, you need to return to your old discipline within a few days. If the change in his sleeping circumstances is temporary, you need to return to your old routine as soon as you return home.

 *Fact*

Don't be surprised, though, if there is some carryover of his fears even after you return home from vacation to familiar surroundings. After all, he doesn't understand why he just spent the last three nights or two weeks in a strange place, and he can't feel secure that it won't happen again.

If you let him, your baby will take advantage of your leniency and continue to insist on your staying with him until he falls asleep or whatever other accommodations you have been making during a vacation or immediately after a move. Without being cruel and lacking understanding, you need to exert discipline and return him to his regular routine.

If your baby, who was sleeping through the night before the vacation or move, continues to wake up during the night even after you return home or after he has had time to get used to the new surroundings, it may be that he's having bad dreams. He may be dreaming of being lost or abandoned. Soothe him, but then put him back to bed in his own crib. Honor his fears, but then be firm. Show him you're there, he has not been abandoned, and it was only a dream, but then put him back in his crib.

## Chapter 10

# Naptime

When your baby is an infant, he will sleep and wake in cycles around the clock, sleeping for several hours and then being awake for several hours. But by somewhere around four months of age, he will be down to two or three naps per day, and by around six months of age, when his sleep becomes consolidated, he'll be taking one morning nap and one afternoon nap. You'll be better able to determine the times of these naps.

## *The Benefits of Napping*

Ask any mom and she'll tell you that kids who nap tend to be less fussy and difficult. Even adults, when we're tired, get grouchy and irritable. Isn't it tougher to make decisions? Aren't you short of patience? Don't things "get to you" more easily? Children who don't nap easily become tired and sleepy. When children are tired and sleepy, they're fussy, difficult, and more obstinate, such as being unwilling to eat strained peas or cereal or trying a new food, or resisting being put into their jackets to go out or even into their pajamas to go to bed—the very thing they need.

Kids who nap also have longer attention spans than kids who don't. This is more observable in a one-year-old than in a six-month-old. But that six-month-old needs her sleep just as badly as the one-year-old does, and napping is an important part of sleeping. In infants who haven't yet consolidated their sleep, much of their sleeping is napping of sorts.

### Work at Home

With an increasing number of folks working at home, Baby's naptime has become a valuable time resource. From secretaries to executives, people have fit their earning schedule into their baby's schedule to the advantage of both. Whether you utilize Baby's naptime as a time for work, a nap of your own, dinner preparation, sewing, paying bills, making phone calls, or whether you simply curl up with a good book and relax, there's no denying what a respite it is when you don't have to cope with a fussy baby or keep an eye out for a crawler or toddler who's forever getting into things.

### Preventing Naps

Occasionally, the parent of a child who is resistant to bedtime or who is docile about being put in the crib but then seems to have difficulty falling asleep will attempt to withhold naps in the hope that doing so will help the child go to sleep better at night. This is a mistake. First, withholding baby's nap in the hope of getting him to sleep more easily at night may well be defeating the purpose. If the baby is overtired by bedtime, which will very likely be the case if he hasn't napped all day, he is going to have more trouble falling asleep, not less.

In addition, babies need their naps for good health and growth. Napping is an important part of sleeping for young children. Napping and sleeping help bolster a good resistance to disease, foster growth, and keep the child in a better frame of mind emotionally.

### Ⓔ *Fact*

Once your child reaches the age of five or six, if he is still napping, you can try to keep him awake all day and put him into bed earlier to compensate. At this age, withholding his nap is not injurious, and he'll soon be in school, where napping won't be an option. So he'd better get adjusted to staying awake through the day.

## How Long and How Many?

Your baby's naps may be one to three hours in duration. Again, please remember that "typical" is not the same as "normal," and if your baby's pattern is different from what's typical, that does not indicate a problem. Somewhere around the age of fifteen to twenty-four months, most babies give up their morning nap. The afternoon nap usually persists until at least between four and six.

 **Alert!**

Napping appreciably longer than three hours calls for some investigation. Discuss the matter with your pediatrician.

Let your baby choose when to give up her morning nap. Don't be the one to decide for her. If you find that you're putting her to bed for her morning nap but she's not going to sleep or that she isn't exhibiting her usual signs of sleepiness beforehand, it may be time to stop offering her the opportunity for a morning nap. A baby's nap needs vary from individual to individual and an evolving thing. Don't change your schedule until you see a definite pattern emerging. A newborn needs three naps a day, and a one-year-old will be down to one or two naps, usually midmorning and early afternoon. By one to two years, most kids need a single nap in the early afternoon.

It may not happen all at once. She may need that nap some days and not other days, and this is fine. Watch her for signs and signals. If on one day she seems to want or need a nap, put her to bed for one. If on other days she seems fine without it, let her stay up. If she skips the morning nap but seems sleepy, fussy, or cranky earlier than the hour at which she had been taking her afternoon nap or you have to give an earlier or much longer afternoon nap, then that would be a good sign that the morning nap was given up too soon.

As she grows older, slowly she will work her way toward getting all her sleep at night, but this happens slowly and in stages, not all at once.

 **Fact**

For reasons science isn't sure of, morning naps feature more REM sleep (active sleep), while afternoon naps consist primarily of more non-REM sleep (quiet sleep). This is true even when the child gives up the morning nap.

## How Naptime Differs from Nighttime

You do not need to go through your usual bedtime routine at naptime. Though your typical nighttime routine may consist of bathing your baby, feeding your baby, singing to her, talking to her, playing a quiet game with her, or some combination of some of these elements, it is not necessary to do this at naptime. If you wish, you can certainly sing one song or talk to her briefly in a soothing voice, but you do not need to do even that. You can simply tell her that it's naptime, offer her a bottle or your breast, and put her in her crib with the blinds drawn and the room darkened.

It's not necessary to put her into her pajamas to nap, but some of the other conditions she associates with sleeping should be present at naptime. The fact that she's in her crib is the biggest signal. Also you will want to close her blinds to shut out the sunlight and much of the daylight, though of course her room won't be totally dark, nor do you need it to be. As well, you will probably nurse her or give her a bottle right before you put her in, as you also do at night.

## Ⓔ *Fact*

Our internal clocks—yours, your baby's, everyone's—are dependent on the regular alternation of light and dark. Left in a perpetually light or perpetually dark room, a person's sleep-regulatory mechanism would soon get disrupted and so would his or her sleep patterns.

### Light and Dark

Experts' opinions are divided as to whether your baby should be put in for her nap in a darkened room or not. Those who say "yes" reason that your baby is learning to associate darkness with sleeping, and so darkening the room is a cue to the baby that she's expected to sleep. Those who say "no" reason that your baby should learn the difference between day and night and not have her body confused by "artificial darkness" at naptime. The best answer is probably a compromise. Put her in her crib for her nap in subdued light, but not in total darkness. It's hard to achieve total darkness in the daytime without the use of blackout shades or heavy drapes.

### Location, Location, Location

In any case, she should be put to sleep in her crib whenever possible. She may fall asleep in her swing or some other place in advance of the time you had planned to put her in her crib for her nap. There's no reason to get upset should this happen. Let her sleep undisturbed so you don't disrupt her sleeping pattern. But when possible, do put her in her crib for her nap. Let her get used to associating the crib with sleeping.

There are several reasons that it's better if the baby naps in her crib, where she sleeps at night. For one thing, she already associates her crib with sleeping. If you put her in for her naps there, she's more likely to get the idea that it's time to go to sleep. In addition, if she is in the thick of daytime household activities, the excessive noise might interrupt her nap. If she's napping in her swing, in her car seat perched on the floor, or on a quilt spread out on the living room floor, she may be more easily awakened by the sound of the doorbell or phone, by the voices of visitors or family members, or by whatever activities are going on around her.

## *Establishing Naptimes and Feeding Times*

You can schedule his naps for times that mesh well with the hours he sleeps at night. What time in the morning does he usually show signs of needing a nap? That would be a good time to schedule it. Try to put him to bed for his morning nap at a consistent time every day.

## Ⓔ *Essential*

When you're deciding what the best time is for your baby's afternoon nap, keep in mind the fact that you want him awake at least four hours after he wakes from his afternoon nap before you put him in for the night. Think of how long he naps, work backward and do the math, and plan the time you'll put him to bed for his nap for a time no later than that.

In planning your baby's afternoon nap, a combination of factors will determine the time you schedule it, including what time he wakes from his morning nap, what time in the afternoon he usually shows signs of sleepiness, and what time he goes to bed at night.

The times at which you'll feed him may have to be adjusted to mesh with his sleeping schedule. As an infant, he'll still be feeding right before he naps and right before you put him in for the night. When you start him on rice cereal or other solid food, you'll want to plan that meal for at least an hour before his bedtime. So, his bedtime is the first consideration; naptimes and feeding times follow. Of course, his getting-up time will be of his body's own choice; when he's had enough sleep, he'll wake up, unless he's awakened earlier by the bustling around of other members of the household.

## *Promoting Good Nap Habits*

Though you want your baby to sleep well during his naptime, don't hush all noise in the house during his naptime, either. To begin with, it probably isn't even feasible. If you live in an area where there's daytime traffic or other street noises, there may be passing cars, truck horns, kids playing in the street, garbage trucks, and other sounds coming in through the windows. In the second place, there will be noise within the house as well. The phone is likely to ring and perhaps the doorbell, too. If you have an older child, perhaps a toddler or three- or four-year-old, he's likely to play noisily, call "Mom!" from one room to the next, turn on the TV to watch his favorite program, run loudly toward the bathroom, or otherwise keep the house from being silent. You, too, may make some noise of your own. You're likely to have music or the TV on, make phone calls while you have some peace and quiet, clatter around in the kitchen, perhaps even run the vacuum, the sewing machine, or some other equipment that raises the decibel level in the house.

All this is good. To begin with, it will differentiate daytime naps from nighttime sleep, when the house and the outdoors are quieter. Second and just as important, it will get your baby accustomed to sleeping through noise.

So go ahead—run the blender or the food processor, the vacuum or the sewing machine, the television or the stereo. Let your older child turn on the television, and if she wants to sing along with Barney or Oscar the Grouch at the top of her lungs, let her, as long as she's not in or right outside the baby's room. Let the noise proceed as usual! Let the phone ring as always, and don't hush your voice when you're on a phone call. You can stop your older child from going into the baby's room and yelling. This is particularly relevant if the baby is sharing a room with his older sibling, who, at 2½ years of age, is intent on running into the room to retrieve a toy while calling out to you and is mindless of the fact that the baby is sleeping in there. But while you wouldn't want to vacuum in the baby's room while he sleeps, don't plunge the house into total silence, either.

### Fact

If you want your baby to be the lightest sleeper on the block, hush everyone up when he's napping, turn off the stereo, and mute the phone. Put a note on the front door: DON'T RING BELL. BABY SLEEPING. You'll soon have a baby who's used to sleeping in total quiet . . . and wakes up at the slightest noise!

### Safety

A too-common practice is that of parents who lie down on the sofa with their babies in the hope that both can nap. It's understandable. But it's not safe. You've had a rough night. The baby kept you up. You're falling asleep.

You've put him in his crib, but he won't nap—in fact, all he'll do is scream. You feel like you can't keep your eyes open another minute; yet you can't get the baby to close his eyes. In desperation you lie on the sofa, wedge the baby between you and the back cushion, give him a bottle, and gratefully close your eyes.

Wake up! You've just placed your baby in an unsafe position. What are the hazards?

- If the baby is old enough to crawl, he can crawl across you while you sleep and can then fall onto the floor. If he doesn't get hurt in the fall, he can still get into something dangerous while you sleep unaware.
- The baby can get wedged between you and the back of the sofa, get his face pushed into the cushions, be unable to cry out, and be smothered.
- You can roll over in your sleep and wedge him badly with his face in the cushions or roll on top of him and smother him yourself.

The hazard factor is even greater if the adult sleeping with the baby is overtired, drunk, obese, drowsy from medications, or any combination of these things.

It's best not to put the baby down for a nap on your bed either—at least, not unless you're used to cosleeping and have set the bedroom up for cosleeping safety. But if you leave the baby on your bed, there are three potential hazards:

- He might roll over and roll off the bed. You say he's never yet rolled over? There's always the first time.
- He might work his way up to your pillow and get smothered by it.
- He might work his way to where he can get wedged between the mattress and the headboard or footboard.

His crib is his napping place. If he's fallen asleep in his car seat or swing and you're sure he'll wake up if you take him out to put him in his crib, you can consider leaving him where he is, though it's not recommended. But don't let him sleep on the couch, with or without you, or on your bed unless it's set up for cosleeping.

## Napping Problems

In the real world, naptime may not always be the scene of perfection we see on television or the movies. Human beings just aren't made that way. A baby may decide one day "I just don't feel like a nap" or "Who needs a three-hour nap, anyway?" Babies also refuse to tell time, read the baby experts' opinions, or decide to make your life easier. They'll sometimes just refuse to get to sleep, wake up after five or ten minutes, get sleepy an hour early, and do anything they can think of to screw up your bedtime routine.

The golden rule here is to stay flexible. You just can't tell a baby what she is and isn't supposed to do. If a baby decides it's time for a trip to "nappieland" in the middle of feeding, off she'll go without buying a ticket from you.

Here's how to handle seemingly difficult situations and keep your cool.

### What If Baby Doesn't Want to Nap?

Try holding and rocking her for awhile, talk or sing gently, or do any of the routine things you do to get her to sleep at night. If it doesn't work and she gets upset, just skip it and go on with her day as if nothing happened. If the crying becomes excessive in length or volume, investigate the possible internal and external reasons.

### What If Baby Wakes Up after Five or Ten Minutes?

Do you end the nap or put him back down? Usually, if a baby wakes up, she thinks, "Well, that was a nice nap. Now I'll go on to something else." She doesn't have a watch to tell her she wasn't asleep long enough. Trying to get her back to "sleepyland" probably won't work, but you can try.

### What If She Gives Up Naps Too Soon?

Do you try a quiet time? Yes. That's what preschools do. They have all sorts of built-in sleep schedules and also one-shot schedules. They let them lie quietly, read books, or play with dolls. This is a transition to full-scale activities. You can do the same by reading and/or playing with your baby. Your baby may want to jump full blown into daytime activities—go for it.

### What If He Wakes Up Very Grumpy?

Do you give him a cooldown period before taking him out of his crib? Most parents would consider that mean. There are some people who bound out of bed and greet the day with a sunshine smile and those who . . . well, don't. You know who you are. Why should a baby be any different? Treat the grump with good will, toleration, and a big smile.

### What If He Misses a Nap?

Do you keep him awake until the next nap or let him take his second nap earlier, which will likely disrupt your bedtime routine? A baby won't ask your permission to take a nap. Trying to keep a baby awake is self-defeating—it will interfere with nighttime sleep, just the thing you want to avoid. The only problem is napping too close to bedtime. That you want to avoid by carefully planning nap times earlier in the day.

## No Substitute for Nighttime Sleep

Napping is an adjunct to sleeping. It is not a substitute. Babies need both. If your baby didn't sleep well last night, a good nap today is an essential. A good nap is an essential under any circumstances until she's three or older. But don't think she can readily get by regularly with a few hours of sleep a night because she is napping well during the day. Your baby needs both naps and night sleep.

The patterns of REM sleep and non-REM sleep are different when sleeping at night than they are when sleeping by day, which tells us that the sleep derived from a nap is in some ways different from the sleep we get at night. Though both are important and one can help make up for the lack of the other, neither is a real replacement for the other. Your baby needs both. You need to see that he gets them.

### Adult Naptime

For a while, until he learns to sleep at night and stay awake by day, you may need to do some of your sleeping by day as well. If you have a toddler at home or if you're already back to work at an outside job, this may be difficult. Even if you're a stay-at-home parent or still out on maternity leave from your job and you have no other children, the doorbell and phone may preclude your getting all the sleep you need by day. Just get as much sleep as you can by night and as much napping as you can by day, take turns with your spouse in staying up at night with the baby when necessary, and get through it as best you can.

### Dealing with Naptime in a Family Bed

Naptime is another time when a family bed baby may insist on your lying down with her before she'll go to sleep. If you've been yawning and feeling drowsy, longing for a nap for quite some time yourself, lying down for a snooze with Baby may be just the most appealing thing.

But if you have a toddler to watch, a mound of ironing you want to get out of the way while Baby is safely out of reach of the iron, or dinner to get started, you may not want to spend from one to three hours asleep on the bed. Even if you do take a nap yourself, it's likely to not last the duration of your baby's nap. Some family bed parents solve this problem by putting their baby to sleep for her nap in her swing or even in her car seat, in whatever room the mom or dad is in. Is it a perfect solution? No. Is it a workable solution? Yes. Will it work for you, if you have a family bed sleeping arrangement? Try it and find out.

## Chapter 11

# Good Morning!

How and when does your baby wake up? With you, ahead of you, or after you? Groggy, bright-eyed, or fussy? Like the rest of us, babies are different from each other in their waking-up habits. Some babies wake up early, eager for the day, gurgling and cooing, or eager for food, howling loudly. Other babies are slow to wake up, are groggy when they do, and aren't in the best frame of mind.

## *Babies Who Wake Up Groggy*

If your baby is waking up groggy, the first thing to do is figure out whether your baby is simply not a morning person or whether she's not getting enough sleep.

Ask yourself: Does your baby wake up on her own or only after other members of the family are up and about? If she's sleeping lightly, as many people do when they're nearing the end of their night's sleep, she may be more easily awakened by a noise than she will be by a similar noise at 10:00 P.M. The TV in the living room that doesn't bother her in the evening may bother her at 6:00 A.M., even if it's on at a lower volume while you listen to the morning news. Having the radio on with its traffic and weather reports as you're getting dressed or sipping coffee could also be the culprit.

Sleeping lightly as she is, the noise more readily wakes her than it would in the evening. In addition, there's probably constant household noise in the background as she's lying in her crib falling asleep, and it continues through the evening. The volume may vary. The type of noise may vary—TV or stereo, voices or the ringing phone, even a siren going by in the street—but there's been some sort of noise. Overnight, though, it's been quiet. Now, in the early morning, suddenly there's noise again, and occurring after a long period of silence, it's more likely to disturb her slumber.

She's even more likely to be awakened if the noise is in the same room. If her crib is in a room with her older sibling, the sound of her sister getting out of bed, perhaps calling to you or opening her dresser drawers or her closet to remove clothes can easily awaken the baby. If her crib is in your room, the sound of your alarm clock, of you and your spouse opening drawers and the closet, perhaps showering in a bathroom that's off the bedroom, perhaps jangling jewelry as you select a pair of earrings, or perhaps talking to each other, no matter how low your voices, can also awaken her easily enough.

## Ⓔ *Essential*

If you simply try to put a baby to sleep earlier, you might have a hard time getting her to sleep before she is ready, and she may not sleep any longer in the morning. Slowly changing a baby's sleep schedule is discussed in Chapter 2.

Do a little detective work: Does she wake up groggy but wake up only after other family members are up and about? She may not be getting enough sleep. A good test would be to make sure that you don't wake her up so that she is allowed to wake up naturally. Evaluate the mood she is in when she wakes up. If that isn't feasible, try putting her to bed half an hour earlier or even an hour earlier. If she then wakes up a half hour or an hour earlier and still wakes up groggy, you'll know that's not the answer. Try to have a consistent morning routine, and give her a little time to fully wake up in her crib before you go to her. If all of this doesn't work, you're simply dealing with a baby who's not a morning person and is going to be slow to wake up no matter how much sleep she's had. You can come to that same conclusion without adjusting her bedtime if she normally wakes up first in the family yet is groggy nonetheless. Also, how long your baby stays grumpy means something. If she wakes up grumpy, but quickly gets into a good mood, she's probably gotten enough sleep.

## Handling a Groggy Baby

What if your baby is one of those babies who wakes up groggy no matter what? What should you do then? First, keep your initial approach to him low-key. Don't bound into the room all cheery and ready to play games with him. He's not ready for that yet. He's still slowly waking up. Though he's not asleep, he's not fully alert. Be respectful of his sensibilities and talk softly to him as you enter the room.

Stroke his head or arm or back or neck and talk to him. Pick him up and hold him. Kiss him, snuggle him, and then, perhaps while you still hold him, let a little light into the room. If it's full daylight out, why not turn on a lamp first and let him get used to that light before you open the blinds or drapes? Tilt the blinds open but don't pull them up yet. Give him a chance to get adjusted. Mornings are tougher for some of us than for others. You may be a morning person, but he isn't. Let him accept the morning slowly.

Change his diaper. Surely feeling fresh and clean will help him feel more wide awake. Then offer him a bottle or your breast, and let him wake up further as he feeds.

Talk to him as he's feeding. Engage him. He may seem to be fully involved with his morning milk intake, but rest assured he's listening to you nonetheless.

If you are offering him solid food first, carry him quietly into the kitchen or dining room and talk or sing as you go, without rushing. If he senses haste and urgency, it could unnerve him.

After his breakfast, dress him or bathe him first and then dress him. Did you bathe him last night? Was his diaper so messy that he needs another bath? Did he play with the bottle and get milk all over himself? Did he eat his strained peaches so messily that bathing him seems preferable to a sponge bath with a washcloth?

By now he should be quite wide awake, and his blinds should be fully opened, although if it's winter and the sun isn't up yet continue to leave on the lamp. But if for any reason he isn't fully awake, a game is a great way to wake him up.

Peek-a-boo can be stimulating, depending on how it's played. Are you merely hiding your face behind your hands, or covering his eyes with your hands, or are you crouching down out of sight and then springing up into his line of vision? The latter is more stimulating, as long as he doesn't startle easily. Even "This Little Piggy" can be stimulating if you run your fingers all up and down his body on the line "Wheee, wheee, wheee, all the way home" and raise your voice excitedly. It's not only your choice of game, but it's also how you choose to play it.

By now your baby should be wide awake, but if he isn't, how about some stimulating music to get him going?

Surely you have a music source either in his room or in the living room—a radio, a CD player, or a tape player? Whether you choose children's music, classical music, rock, or something else that suits your sensibilities, it will help energize your baby and get him on course for greeting the day with a sunnier disposition.

## Babies Who Are Early Risers

On the other hand, the problem may be not that she wakes up groggy but simply that she is a morning person and therefore wakes up earlier than you and your spouse care to be awakened. Yet there's Baby, calling to you from her crib, so what choice do you have? Though you can try adjusting her to a later bedtime in the hope that she'll sleep later as a result, you may find that she wakes up early anyhow and hasn't had enough sleep. She's simply a morning person who just naturally wakes up early. There are several things you can try in dealing with early risers. Make sure the room stays dark and quiet, put her back to bed after a quick feeding, or let her fuss a little. If these suggestions fail, revert to the earlier bedtime. Make sure she gets enough sleep. If she still is up with the roosters, you've got a "lark" for a baby.

Is food the first thing she wants when she wakes up? Does she cry for you not because she's hungry but because now that she's awake she's bored and wants something to do? Here's another experiment to try: Leave a toy in the crib, something it's safe for her to sleep with, that has no sharp corners or other hazards, but something that will intrigue her when she wakes up. See if, instead of crying, she coos as she discovers the toy and then busily plays with it for a while.

## Fact

There are two reasons you might want your baby to learn to sleep later. One is to insure that she's getting enough sleep. The other is so that you can sleep later. If she's getting enough sleep despite arising early and if she learns to play quietly by herself without crying when she first wakes up, it's no longer a problem if she awakens at an early hour.

If she wakes at 5:30 A.M. and plays with the toy, she may even settle down and go back to sleep after a bit, but if not, it's not a problem, as long as she's not getting you up. At first, you may wake up on hearing the crib creak and your baby coo, especially if she's in the same room as you. But after a few days of realizing that she's not winding up for a full-throated yowl, you'll probably roll over and go right back to sleep, if indeed you wake up at all, when Baby wakes up and finds her toy and begins playing. Just be careful in your choice of crib toy—don't choose anything she can hurt herself with if she rolls onto it during the night.

## When Baby Is Wide Awake

Sooner or later, your baby is going to want you. Whether she wants food, company, a distraction, or all of these, she's going to call for you. Of course, at her age, that means crying.

### First Things First

You'll want to change her diaper, of course, though she may be intent on feeding and may howl through the diaper-changing process. If you're bottle-feeding her, you can accomplish both simultaneously, bringing her a bottle, settling her down on your bed, on her changing table, or in her crib with the side down and changing her diaper while she feeds. If you're nursing her, you can't do it simultaneously with changing her diaper, and she's just going to have to wait until you get the diaper changed. If she's already on cereal or strained food, you may want to offer some of that to her before giving her a bottle or offering her your breast to nurse.

If she's taking a bottle, once you've got her diaper changed, you can hold her while she feeds if you have the time. If she's old enough to hold her own bottle and you're rushing to get dressed, get an older child dressed and fed breakfast, or take care of other morning chores, you can leave her someplace safe to drink her bottle on her own. It's better for two reasons if that place isn't her crib:

- You want her to associate the crib with sleeping. Giving her a breakfast bottle there sends the wrong message.
- It's good if you can interact with her while she feeds. Even if you're not holding her, you can talk to her. If she's in a secure seat such as a car seat, a swing, or

on a quilt in the middle of the floor of whatever room you're in, you can talk to her as you get dressed, make breakfast, or do other tasks.

As she drinks her bottle, or eats her breakfast, or nurses at your breast, she'll become more awake (if she didn't awaken wide-awake at first). If she awakened all agitated because she was once again, as always, confined to her crib and hungry, the bottle or breast will soothe her even while waking her up. A nice bath, though also soothing, can as well be energizing, and you can play with her while she's in the water, splishing and splashing (carefully!) and letting her have fun. It's giggle time, and isn't that grand?

Then, whether you bathe your baby in the morning or not, it's time to get her dressed. "Dressed" may mean pants and a shirt, or a dress, or a "onesies," or whatever other outfit is appropriate, but get her ready for the day and, unless you're leaving the house with her right away, try to spend a little time playing with her. Get her in a good mood. We all like to start out our mornings on the right foot, and babies are no different.

### Don't Rush

If you have limited time in the morning, get up early enough, and be sure that your baby gets up early enough so that you can get her through the early morning's activities without rushing her.

You may need to get up a half hour earlier. You may need to get Baby to bed a half hour earlier so that she wakes up a half hour earlier, too. You may mourn the lost sleep. But which is worse? To lose a half hour's sleep and have a peaceful morning or to sleep that extra half hour but have a hurried, harried, hassled start to your day, with you feeling impatient with Baby and clashing with her because she's dawdling at your breast or playing with her cereal or not cooperating when you try to dress her? You'll both feel the strain. You'll both feel rushed. You'll be at odds with each other. You'll get the day off to a bad start for both of you. Is this worth a half hour's sleep? The luxury of sleeping in a half hour longer is more than offset by the calm you gain by getting an earlier start.

### E Alert!

If you're hurried and hassled and you're feeding Baby cereal or strained food, you may grow impatient if she eats slowly, balks at eating, or does anything but eat her food with dispatch and efficiency. This sets up a negative connection in her mind with eating, which is not what you want. This is another reason for leaving plenty of time in the morning.

## Subtle Methods for Waking Up Baby

What if you have to wake Baby up? What if it's 7:00 a.m., he's not awake yet, and you need to get him ready to go to the babysitter's or the day care facility, or need to get him ready to go out with you as you make your daily rounds, or drop your older child at the day care center, or whatever your needs are? What if he's sleeping late and that doesn't work with your plans for the day? What if it's an unusual day, when Mom or Dad has to catch an early flight for a business trip and needs a ride to the airport? What if you have a meeting and need to get to work an hour earlier? How are you going to wake Baby up?

### Create an "Awake" Environment

First, walk quietly into his room and open his blinds. If it's 5:00 A.M. in winter, opening the blinds isn't going to make a bit of difference. But if it's 7:00 A.M. in summer, the sunlight will come streaming in. If sunlight or simply sufficient daylight doesn't reach the windows in question at the hours you need it, turn on a light in his room.

Turn on some music, too, if you want. Turn up the volume on the radio or TV in some other room, though music in your baby's room will be more effective. Hum or sing along with the music. Create light. Create noise. If all else fails (though that's hardly likely), stroke your baby's legs or arms or face, as you talk directly to her over the bars of the crib.

She'll wake up. If she's not a morning person, she's going to be groggy or maybe even cross. Have a bottle ready or be ready to nurse or have some strained fruits or vegetables or some cereals ready, if she's old enough. But be prepared to talk to her and keep her occupied while she feeds at the bottle or breast. Otherwise, if she wasn't ready to wake up yet, she might go back to sleep while she's feeding. Try to engage her as she suckles at the bottle or breast.

Having activity around her will help her wake up as well. Get her diaper changed, get her dressed, and get her out into the living room or kitchen or dining room— somewhere where other family members are located. Let her get intrigued with what the other family members are doing. Let her get involved. Let her wake up as she follows the activities of others. Then get her ready for the day at hand. Are you about to take her out on a car ride? Tell her excitedly that's she's going in the car! She's going for a ride! Are you about to drive to the airport? Tell her she's going to see the planes! Keep excitement in your voice.

## Ⓔ *Essential*

If you're playing or singing music, pick fast songs ("Pop Goes the Weasel" rather than "The Farmer in the Dell") or a more up-tempo album rather than a mellow one.

### This Little Massaged Piggy

Another tactic to take with babies who are reluctant to wake up is a brisk foot massage. Taking care not to rub so hard that you cause friction and burning (an application of a little baby oil will help prevent that), rub her feet briskly. Rub either front-to-back and back up again or side-to-side and back again. Use your whole hand. Although you're rubbing briskly, don't bear down hard on your baby's sensitive foot. This foot massage will help her to wake up. Brisk but restrained arm massage is also helpful.

## Chapter 12

# Making Up for Lost Time . . . and Sleep (Yours)

You've tried all the strategies in this book to get your baby to sleep. But babies, as you well know, are not programmable, and there are going to be times when your baby just won't sleep. Something is keeping him awake, and therefore, you are also kept awake. There you are sleepy but sleepless, frustrated, and at your wits' end. What are you going to do?

## Coping When Baby Won't Sleep

When your baby is awake in the middle of the night, you're going to do everything you can think of to make him more comfortable and help him get back to sleep. If he's an infant new to this world, there may be no specific problem. He's simply awake at an inappropriate time, not sleepy as you'd like him to be, and there's nothing to do but to stay up with him until he goes back to sleep or at least is willing to lie quietly in his crib. If he doesn't seem hungry or he's just nursed or had a bottle and still is awake, chalk it up to the sleep irregularities of infancy. Resign yourself to being awake for a few hours.

### E Essential

Playing with your baby is not a good idea. Not only do you not want him to get revved up, but you also want him to learn that nighttime is quiet time and that nighttime is for sleeping. Don't send him the wrong signals by engaging him in a game. Talk to him. Sing to him. Hold him and snuggle him. Rock him or walk with him. But now is not the time for peek-a-boo or "This Little Piggy" or "Where Is Thumbkin?"

You can try rocking him, walking with him, or any of the other things suggested in this book, and one of them might work. But there's also a good chance that he's simply going to be awake for a while, maybe even for several hours. Think of it as spending some more precious time with your baby (soon enough you'll wonder when he grew up so fast) and make the best of it. If you let yourself get frustrated at his wakefulness and your resultant inability to sleep, you'll only grow angry at him and also become so agitated that, even when he finally does go back to sleep, you'll be unable to drift off yourself.

Better to relax and rest as best you can, perhaps in your rocking chair, with your baby in one arm and a good book in the other hand. If you can put on some soft, relaxing music without waking anyone else, go ahead and do it. Even if it doesn't do anything for your baby, you need to relax.

You may find that you feel better about being awake if you accomplish something. Perhaps you can hold him in the crook of one arm while using your other hand to make out a grocery list. If you're a hunt-and-peck typist rather than a touch typist and typing with only one hand won't bother you, use the opportunity to get on the computer and answer e-mail, visit that Web site you've been meaning to check out, or download some new recipes. Write up that letter you owe your mother. How about sending out some thank-you notes for baby gifts? If you still owe some thank-yous, now would be a good time to write them.

If you can't sleep, the next best thing is to be productive. Then you won't feel quite as bad about being awake for a while. At least you'll have accomplished something meaningful with your time. If you don't work outside the home, or you're still on maternity leave, or are working from home, you can try to catch a nap during the day. Just as with babies, adult naps don't totally make up for lost sleep at nighttime. But they sure go a long way toward helping.

## Conflicting Schedules

Unless your situation is unusual, in his first few weeks or months your baby will wake up often during the night and not always go back to sleep after he's been fed. It isn't easy, but it's what's normal for babies. There's nothing wrong with him. You and your spouse and any other members of your family have some rough nights ahead. It's normal to be disappointed, to be frustrated, and to be sleepy. You want seven or eight hours of solid sleep in a night. Your baby has other ideas.

If you're already back to work and not working from a home office or if you're parenting one or more other children, you may not be able to nap on and off through the day when your baby does. Even if there are no other kids and no job to require you to stay awake all day, the phone, household chores, doorbell, or your Things To Do list may not let you nap. But if you understand that a baby who wakes in the middle of the night may be up for two hours or perhaps even longer, you may be better prepared to accept this behavior on his part.

## Getting Your Husband Involved

Even in the old days when dads were less involved in childrearing than they are now, many fathers recognized their responsibilities when it came to babies who cried in the middle of the night. Fathers through the ages have paced the floor with their little ones on their shoulders, trying to calm the crying.

Nursing moms are at a bit of a disadvantage; it's harder to get Dad to cover the 2:00 A.M. feeding. But that doesn't let Dad totally off the hook.

- Mom can leave some breast milk in a bottle in the fridge in advance of the 2:00 A.M. feeding, which Dad can then offer the baby while Mom sleeps.
- Dad can feed formula to the baby on occasion so that Mom can sleep through a middle-of-the-night feeding.
- Mom can get up to take care of the feeding, but then let it be Dad's turn if Baby won't go back to sleep after nursing or if Baby wakes up again a little while later and presumably isn't hungry again so soon.

Don't plead. Don't beg. It makes it seem like you're asking him for a favor. It's not a favor. This is his child, his baby, as much his child as yours and as much his responsibility as yours. Not only should he get up and take the baby from her crib some of the times she's crying in the middle of the night, but if you've been up with her for an hour or two and she's not ready to go back to sleep yet, rouse your husband from his sleep and tell him it's his turn; you're tired from walking the floor, you're sleepy, and he can take over for the next hour or two or until she goes back to sleep.

### Subtle Communication

In the meanwhile, send him signals and learn to read his. Leave him alone in the crib when he's awake in the middle of the night if he's not crying. If he's merely cooing but not upset and setting up a fuss, there's no reason to pick him up. He can lie there and make noises. Let him be. His sounds may keep you awake, but you can read, listen to music, watch TV, or get something accomplished until he goes back to sleep or until he erupts into crying. You might even try lying down and resting. His cooing may keep you from sleeping, but you can still relax. If he's not crying, there's no reason to get on edge.

Learn the ways this book teaches you to soothe him to sleep so that eventually he goes back to sleep and you can get back to sleep, too. Send him signals such as talking in a quiet voice, not playing, and not turning the lamps on brightly so that he knows that daytime is for being awake and that the night is for sleeping. Be aware of his signals, too.

You've already learned about signals to watch for that will indicate he is growing sleepy. Babies have their own language. It isn't verbal. But you and he can communicate with each other.

## Crying It Out

The hotly contested question of whether to let a baby "cry it out," that is, to cry herself to sleep, has settled down to one of degree. Babies cry for a reason. Parents should attempt to find out what that reason is and correct it. But once you have gone through the list presented earlier in this book and Baby is still wailing away, just do your best to comfort her, put her back into the crib, and wait for her to fall asleep. If this is a recurrent thing and Baby cries routinely for hours, alert your pediatrician. Chances are there is nothing medically wrong, but you must always err on the cautious side when it comes to your child.

## Ⓔ *Essential*

While your baby lies in his crib and cries and screams, not only will he be miserable, but also you won't feel any too happy yourself. You know all that yowling will set your nerves on edge. You certainly won't get back to sleep. Your spouse will be awakened too, along with any other members of the household. Use this as a last resort, when nothing else is working.

### Helping You Help Yourself

Better to accept that there are going to be periods of wakefulness during the night in Baby's early months, especially during the first weeks, and that you're going to lose sleep. Better to get something accomplished, read a good book, or relax as best you can until Baby is tired and ready to go back to sleep. He won't be up all night. Babies of that age almost never stay awake for eight-hour stretches. What are some of the things you can do to help yourself with your sleep deprivation?

- Go to bed when you put Baby in for the evening, even if it's at 7:00 P.M. If you can't go to sleep for the night at that hour, at least lie down and take a nap.

- Take as many naps as you can during the day when Baby is napping.
- Enlist the aid of others to watch Baby and give you a respite.
- Accept that when Baby is napping during the day that it's more important that you nap rather than that you get the house clean or get a lavish or complex dinner cooked.
- Rest as much as possible, even when you can't sleep.
- If you're sleep-deprived due to Baby being awake at night, rather than overdose on coffee to stay alert, which might keep you awake if Baby suddenly decides to go to sleep and give you an opportunity for a nap, rely on extra showers to wake you up and refresh you. Then you have a better chance at napping if Baby naps.
- Don't focus on how tired you are. It will only make you feel worse.

Don't let your tiredness tempt you into anything risky like lying down on the sofa with the baby on top of you and your arms around him to hold him in place or lying there with the baby wedged between you and the sofa back. No matter how tired you are, don't take such risks!

### Time to Cool It

There is one exception, though, to what we discussed about not putting Baby into her crib to cry it out. If you feel at your wits' end and close to being out of control and you're growing upset and angry with your baby, you're better off to leave her crying inconsolably in the crib than to keep her in your arms and risk doing something harmful to her. The newspapers are full of stories of parents who, driven wild by lack of sleep and/or by the incessant crying of their babies, shook their babies or threw bottles at them or hit them. Certainly, you know that this is not a disciplinary matter. When you're thinking clearly, you know that your baby is not "being bad" or crying out of stubbornness or bad behavior. Certainly you're aware that hitting her, shaking her, or otherwise disciplining her is not only inappropriate, but also dangerous to her. But if you're at the breaking point due to sleeplessness, it's better to put her in her crib and let her howl than to hold her and risk harming her. Leaving her in her crib to cry alone may not be kind, but in this case, it's the lesser of the two evils.

## Finding Support Through Family, Friends, and Babysitters

Do you have a few friends who haven't yet given your baby presents and are asking you what you need? Here's a thought: Tell them, "We have all the clothes and toys for her that we need. What I really need is a break. Some sleep. Some rest. You really want to give us something? Give us some respite. Watch the baby while I take a nap or watch her while we go out for dinner."

Going out for dinner won't help the sleep situation, of course, but it will give you a much-needed break that may be as useful as a few hours of Zzzzs.

Who else can you call on for respite? Do you have relatives—your parents, a sibling—who live in the area? How about enlisting your best friend . . . and a few other friends, too? What about a paid babysitter? None of these is likely to be able to help you overnight. After all, you don't really want to ask your mom, sister, or friend to endure a sleepless night while you slumber peacefully. But they could watch your baby by day while you catch a much-needed nap.

## Ⓔ Essential

The optimal situation is for your rescuer to do some off-premises babysitting, with your relative, friend, or babysitter watching your baby at this person's own house while you sleep at home, blissfully undisturbed. But even if you can't arrange that, just close the door to your room and try to shut out the sound if your baby wakes up and cries. Someone else is there and taking care of Baby.

If you can't arrange for off-premises babysitting, maybe you can arrange for you to be off-premises while your rescuer babysits. While your mom is at your house watching your baby, maybe you can go to your mom's house and sleep there, undisturbed by crying in the next room.

If that's not feasible, maybe another friend would offer you the use of her home or apartment. Do you have a friend who works and isn't home by day? If she has a husband and/or kids, are they gone from the house by day, too? Borrow a key and go stretch out on your friend's bed for some much-needed sleep while your babysitter handles the baby-watching chores back home.

In fact, getting occasional respite care and going off on your own is a good plan even if you don't use the time to catch up on your sleep. Going out to lunch with a friend or your spouse, getting your hair done, wandering through an art gallery, or doing whatever appeals to you recreationally are all fine plans for daytime escapes. But in those first few months, when your sleep may be badly curtailed, getting caught up on sleep is more important than any of those other things and will probably be your primary objective when you can get respite care for the baby.

## Ⓔ *Question?*

**What if my baby gets hungry while I'm gone? I'm breastfeeding.**

Using manual expression or a breast pump, fill a bottle and leave it for the baby in the fridge. Your temporary caregiver can give her the bottle when Baby gets hungry. If you left a bottle of formula instead, that would be okay, too.

Don't be afraid to ask for help, either. Friends may not realize it's what you need most. If your friends all have day jobs away from home and you have no relatives living nearby, pay a sitter and/or ask your friends for help on weekends. On Wednesday morning after a curtailed Tuesday night's sleep, Saturday may seem a long way off, but you'll still be grateful for even just an hour of coverage on Saturday when it comes.

You can even find another woman—a friend, a neighbor, anyone you trust—who has a baby of comparable age and would be willing to trade off with you, with one of you watching both kids and then the other watching both kids, giving each other a chance to sleep.

### Using a Night Nurse

The use of a night nurse to help out with a new baby is a growing trend for those who can afford it. Finding someone to come to your home and take responsibility for your baby calls for careful investigation. Work from the recommendation of a friend or seek help from a reputable nurse's agency. There is usually a minimum and a maximum period specified when working through an agency—typically two weeks to six months, but that will vary and may be subject to negotiation. The cost is significant. Typically, agencies charge between $17.50 and $35.00 an hour for an eight-hour day.

## Don't Blame Yourself . . . or Anyone Else

If the baby isn't a "good sleeper," don't ever become self-recriminating over it. It's not that you're being a bad mother. It's not that you don't know how to get him to sleep. It's not that you're doing anything wrong or failing to do something right. The baby is simply doing what babies do: crying often, sleeping in cycles that don't conform to yours, and demonstrating perfectly normal, natural actions that are in no way the result of any failure or inadequacy on your part.

If your friend had a baby right around the same time you did and your friend's baby gets up once during the night for a bottle and goes right back to sleep, while yours is up for hours on end, don't feel inadequate. Don't feel you must be doing something wrong. Feel envious if you wish. That's entirely appropriate. Your friend is getting a good night's sleep every night, while you're miserable. Envy is totally understandable. Of course, you wish your baby would start sleeping better! But it's not because your friend is a better mother or is doing something right that you're not.

If your husband is failing to shoulder his share of the nighttime brigade chores, blame him for your tiredness if you wish, but the baby's sleeplessness isn't his fault any more than it's your fault or anyone's. It's not because he played with her or talked to her too loudly before bedtime or tiptoed in to see if she was okay.

## Ⓔ *Alert!*

Don't blame the baby, either. Don't say, "She's not good," though you can say "She's not a good sleeper yet." (Hang on to that "yet"—it indicates hope for the future.) Sleeping patterns are not "behavior" in the sense of being "well behaved" or "badly behaved."

It's a natural human trait to want to find a scapegoat, someone or something on which we can place blame when things go wrong. But the only "blame" here falls squarely on nature: It's natural for babies to be awake at night sometimes, to cry, fail to sleep, and drive their parents to the edge of tolerance. It's nobody's fault but nature's—not yours, not your husband's, not that of the friend or pediatrician or other expert whose advice you've been following, and not that of the baby herself. Stuff happens.

So do your best to calm her down, be grateful when she goes back to sleep, make sure your husband does his fair share, and get rest whenever you can. Better days—and nights—are ahead.

## Appendix A

# Additional Resources

## Web Sites

**www.ivillage.com**
This Web site contains articles and message boards on specific parenting topics, including sleepless babies.

**www.forparentsbyparents.com**
A parenting and advice Web site, with a section on sleepless babies.

**www.zerotothree.org**
Billed as "The nation's leading resource on the first years of life." Many articles, message boards, Q & A sections, etc.

**www.warmlines.org**
WarmLines Parent Resources helps families with young children solve typical parenting problems.

**www.parentingonline.org**
Offers both online classes and in-person classes in Idaho.

**www.askdrsears.com**
The Web site of pediatricians William and Martha Sears contains articles and FAQs about sleep problems.

**www.babycenter.com**
BabyCenter's Web site has information about baby sleep, and it even includes lyrics for quite a few lullabies!

**www.medem.com**
Medem maintains an online medical library of AAP articles on children's sleep issues.

## Books

*Sleep the Brazelton Way,* T. Berry Brazelton, M.D., & Joshua D. Sparrow, M.D., Perseus Publishing, 2003.

*Solve Your Child's Sleep Problems,* Richard Ferber, M.D., Fireside, 1985.

*Sweet Dreams,* Paul M. Fleiss, M.D., M.P.H., F.A.A.P., with Frederick M. Hodges, D. Phil., Lowell House, 2000.

*Good Nights,* Jay Gordon, M.D., & Maria Goodavage, St. Martin's Griffin, 2002.

*The Happiest Baby on the Block,* Harvey Karp, M.D., Bantam, 2002.

*Sleeping Through the Night,* Jodi A. Mindell, Ph.D., HarperPerennial, 1997.

*The No-Cry Sleep Solution,* Elizabeth Pantley, Contemporary Books, 2002.

*Sleep Like a Baby,* Avi Sadeh, Yale University Press, 2001.

# Where to Shop for Sleep Products

**One Step Ahead**
☎(800) 274-8440
✎*www.onestepahead.com*

**Right Start Catalog**
☎(800) 548-8531
✎*www.rightstart.com*

# Organizations

**American Sleep Apnea Association**
☎(202) 293-3650
✎*www.sleepapnea.org*

**First Candle/SIDS Alliance**
☎(800) 638-7437
✎*www.sidsalliance.org*

**National Sleep Foundation**
☎(202) 347-3471
✎*www.sleepfoundation.org*

**U.S. Consumer Product Safety Commission**
☎(800) 638-2772
✎*www.cpsc.gov*

## *Appendix B*

# Support Groups

**M**ost parenting support groups are under the auspices of hospitals with obstetrics departments. Contact the hospital in which you had your baby or any other local hospital with a maternity department to ask if they offer a parenting support group or can direct you to one. Though the group will likely not be concerned solely with sleep issues, these do make up a large part of what is discussed in the typical parenting group, especially one geared to parents of babies in particular. Here are three such groups.

**The Center for Childbirth**

✍ *www.valleyhealth.com*

The Valley Hospital

223 N. Van Dien Avenue

Ridgewood, NJ 07450

✆ (201) 447-8403

webinfo@valleyhealth.com

**New Parents Group**

John Muir Medical Center

1601 Ygnacio Valley Rd.

Walnut Creek, CA 94598

✆ (925) 947-3331

**Postpartum Education for Parents (PEP)**

✍ *www.sbpep.org*

pepmail@yahoo.com

PEP was founded in 1977 by a group of mothers to offer each other support after the births of their children. PEP is a nonprofit, all-volunteer corporation staffed entirely by trained parent volunteers.

# Index

## A

abandonment, fear
of, 144, 162
"active sleep" (REM
sleep), 5–6
naps and, 171,
180–181
nightmares and, 39
adenotonsillar
hypertrophy, 46
allergies
to dust, 135
to food, 20
to milk, 31
American Academy of
Pediatrics (AAP), on
cosleeping, 130,
134
anxieties, 35–36
apnea, 42, 44–46
attitude, importance
of positive, 63–64
auditory sleep starts, 44
awakening, 183–194
after short time, 36–37
of early risers, 188–189
grogginess and,
184–188
grumpiness and, 180
how to start the
day, 189–192
how to wake sleeping
baby, 192–194

## B

babysitters
bedtime routine
and, 55
help during day
from, 203–206
back, importance of
sleeping on, 122, 133
back rub, 74
bad dreams. See
nightmares;
night terrors
bassinet, 112–113
baths, 58
bed, moving from
crib to, 148. See
also cosleeping
bedding
blankets, 84, 120–121
mattresses, 108–109,
111–112, 121,
133–134
pillows, 120, 137
sheets, 115–119
see also crib

bedroom
    moving to own,
        123–124, 147–149
    sharing with parents,
        126–127
    sharing with sibling,
        97, 148–149
    *see also* cosleeping
bedtime, 9–10
    establishing routine
        for, 54–62, 69
    falling asleep on
        own, 62, 67–74
    parental attitude
        toward, 63–64
    signs of baby's
        sleepiness, 55–56, 61
biological clock,
    resetting, 26–27
birth order, 15
blame, avoiding, 206–208
blankets
    safety and, 120–121
    warming of, 84
boredom, 35
bottle
    breastfeeding
        versus, 18–19
    falling asleep
        without, 73

breastfeeding
    bottle versus,
        18–19
    cosleeping and,
        129–130
    during night, 199
breathing, sleep
    disturbances and,
        46–49. *See also*
    sleep apnea
bumper pads,
    113–114
burping, 30

## C

car, sleeping in,
    79–80, 158–160
carriage, 81
cereal, 20–21
chin, receding, 46
choking, 47–48
climbing, cribs
    and, 114–115
clothing. *See* nightclothes
colic, 27–29
Consumer Product Safety
    Commission (CPSC)
    breastfeeding and, 129
    cosleeping and,
        130–131, 133

cosleeping, 125–141
  advantages of, 128
  disadvantages
    of, 130–133
  ending of, 140–141
  naps and, 181–182
  nursing and, 129–130
  privacy and, 139–140
  safety and, 133–139
  when traveling,
    151, 157–158
coughing, 47–48
cradle, 79, 112
crib
  bumper pads on,
    113–114
  choosing correct,
    108–111
  climbing hazards
    of, 114–115
  doing without, 151–152
  in hotel, 150–151
  mechanical safety
    and, 116–117
  moving to bed from,
    145–147, 148
  for napping,
    172–173, 178
  in parents' bedroom,
    126–127
  portable, 111–112
  settling baby in, 62–64
  "sidecar," 138–139
  *see also* bedding
crying
  for attention, 84
  as communication,
    68–69
  how to handle,
    200–201
  parental tension and,
    76–77, 202–203

# D

dark
  fear of, 50, 57, 100–101
  naps and, 172–173
day, differentiating
  from night, 5, 7, 8,
  12–13, 27, 64–66
day care, 160–162
diaper pins, 49
diapers, 51, 190
distractions, adjusting
  to, 92–96
Down syndrome, 46
dreams. *See* nightmares;
  night terrors
dust, allergies to, 135

**E**

ear infection, 34
early risers, 188–189

**F**

family, help from, 203–206
family bed. *See* cosleeping
fears
    of abandonment,
        144, 162
    of dark, 50, 57, 100–101
    reacting to, 164–166
feedings, 9, 11, 13–14
    breast versus
        bottle, 18–19
    first thing in morning,
        190–191
    hunger and, 36–37
    nap times and, 173–174
    during night, 199
    on-demand versus
        scheduled, 21–25
    signs of hunger and, 34
    of solid foods, 20–21
    when visiting
        relatives, 155–157
Ferber, Richard, 6
fever, 164
fire-retardant sheets,
    118–120

food, allergies to, 20.
    *See also* feeding
foot massage, 194
friends, help from, 203–206

**G**

games, quiet, 87–88, 187
gas, 30, 35
GERD (Gastro-Esophageal
    Reflux Disease), 48
grogginess, when
    waking, 180, 184–188

**H**

habits, avoiding
    bad, 61–62
head banging, 78
humidity, 50
hunger. *See* feeding
husband, nighttime baby
    care and, 198–199, 207

**I**

illness, 162–164
    night terrors and, 41
    sleep apnea and, 46
    *see also* medications
intestinal distress,
    27–29, 30–31

**J**

jerking (myclonic
    jerks), 43–44

**L**

lactose intolerance, 31
lead-based paint,
    109–110, 136
light
    adjusting to changes
        in, 98, 100–101
    naps and, 172–173
    *see also* day
lullaby, 58–59, 83

**M**

massage, 74, 86–87
mattress
    cosleeping and,
        121, 133–134
    in crib, 108–109
    in portable crib, 111–112
medications, 164
    at bedtime, 60
    night terrors and, 38, 41
    *see also* illness
melatonin, 10–13, 65
mesh-sided cribs/
    playpens, 111

milk, allergies to, 31
mobiles, 63, 88,
    89, 115, 117
monitor, 137
mouth-breathing, 47
music, 89
myclonic jerks, 43–44

**N**

naps, 70, 167–182
    for adults, 181–182
    benefits of, 168–169
    in car, 66, 158
    household sounds and,
        96–99, 175–176
    not substitutes
        for nighttime
        sleep, 180–181
    problems with,
        178–180
    routine and, 171–173
    safety and, 177–178
    timing of, 170–171,
        173–175
new surroundings,
    143–166
    in day care, 160–162
    fears and, 164–166
    at home, 144–149
    with relatives, 154–158

on vacation, 149–154
when sick, 162–164
night
    differentiating from
        day, 5, 7, 8, 12–13,
        27, 64–66
    sleeping through,
        4, 10–13, 71
nightclothes
    fit of, 52
    importance of
        wearing, 58, 63
    materials and, 119–120
night-light, 57, 72, 147
nightmares, 37–38
night nurse, 206
night terrors
    (parasomnias), 37–43
noises. See sounds
non-REM sleep ("quiet
    sleep"), 5–7
    naps and, 171, 180–181
    night terrors and, 39
nurse, for nighttime, 206
nursing. See breastfeeding

O

on-demand versus
    scheduled feeding,
    21–25, 35

overstimulation,
    avoiding before
    bedtime, 55
overtiredness, 56,
    65, 66–67

P

pacifier, 72
paint
    on crib, 109–110
    on parents' bed,
        136
parasomnias (night
    terrors), 37–43
parents
    advice for sleepless,
        195–208
    lack of sleep and
        tension of, 76–77,
        202–203
    spouse as nighttime
        help, 198–199,
        207
    see also cosleeping
pillows, 120, 137
playpens, mesh-sided,
    111
portable crib, 111–112
prayer, at bedtime,
    60

**Q**

quiet games, 87–88

"quiet sleep" (non-REM), 5–7
  naps and, 171, 180–181
  night terrors and, 39

R

recall announcements, 110

receding chin, 46

relatives, visiting of, 154–158

REM sleep, 5–7
  naps and, 171, 180–181
  nightmares and, 39

rocking, 77–79

room. *See* bedroom

room temperature, 49, 85, 104

**S**

safety
  cosleeping and, 133–139
  naps and, 177–178
  paint and, 109–110, 136
  *see also* crib

schedule
  adjusting of, 25–27, 70
  importance of establishing, 9–10
  on-demand versus scheduled feeding, 21–25, 35

self-soothing, 67–74

separation anxiety, 144, 162

sheets, safety and, 115–119

siblings
  sharing bed with, 136
  sharing room with, 97, 148–149

sickness. *See* illness; medications

sidecar crib, 138–139

SIDS (Sudden Infant Death Syndrome), 85, 121–123

singing, 58–59, 82–83

sleep
  early cycles of, 54
  importance of, 2–5
  patterns of, 7–10, 14–16
  sleeping through the night, 4, 10–13, 71

sleep apnea, 42, 44–46

sleepiness, signs of, 55–56, 61

sleepwalking, 39, 42

smoke detectors, 120
smoking, by mother, 123
snoring, 45, 46–47
"snuggle nest," 139
sofa, 121
sounds
    baby's changing
        reaction to, 92–96
    of baby while
        asleep, 13–14
    naptime and,
        96–99, 175–176
    quiet versus loud,
        99–100
    when visiting
        relatives, 154–155
    when waking, 184–185
    white noise machines,
        102–105
spindles, on cribs, 113
storytelling, 59–60, 83
strange place, night
    terrors and, 41
stress, night terrors
    and, 41
suffocation hazards, 115–
    116, 120–121, 131, 135
swaddling, 84–85
swing, 80–81

T
talking, to baby, 82–83
talking in sleep,
    of baby, 48
teething, 29
temperature, of room,
    49, 85, 104
time zone changes,
    152–153
tone of voice,
    59–60, 82–83
travel, 96, 98, 149–154

V
vacation. See travel
visual sleep starts, 44
voice, recognizing
    of, 58–60, 82–83

W
waterbeds, avoiding,
    108, 133
white sound machines,
    102–105

# We Have Everything® ... for Parents

## Parenting Bestsellers

Trade Paperback, $14.95
ISBN: 1-58062-808-7

Trade Paperback, $14.95
ISBN: 1-55850-655-1

Trade Paperback, $15.00
ISBN: 1-58062-336-0

Trade Paperback, $9.95
ISBN: 1-58062-740-4

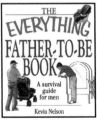

Trade Paperback, $14.95
ISBN: 1-58062-974-1

Trade Paperback, $14.95
ISBN: 1-58062-592-4

From parents-to-be to seasoned pros . . .
we've covered all the stages to help
you from cradle to college.

Everything® Baby Shower Book, $12.95
ISBN: 1-58062-305-0

Everything® Baby's First Food Book, $14.95
ISBN: 1-58062-512-6

Everything® Baby's First Year Book, $14.95
ISBN: 1-58062-581-9

Everything® Birthing Book, $14.95
ISBN: 1-59337-141-1

Everything® Breastfeeding Book, $14.95
ISBN: 1-58062-582-7

Everything® Father's First Year Book, $14.95
ISBN: 1-59337-310-4

Everything® Get Ready for Baby Book, $14.95
ISBN: 1-55850-844-9

Everything® Get Your Baby to Sleep Book, $9.95
ISBN: 1-59337-356-2

Everything® Getting Pregnant Book, $14.95
ISBN: 1-59337-034-2

Everything® Homeschooling Book, $14.95
ISBN: 1-58062-868-0

Everything® Mother's First Year Book, $14.95
ISBN: 1-59337-425-9

Everything® Pregnancy Fitness Book, $14.95
ISBN: 1-58062-873-7

Everything® Pregnancy Nutrition Book, $14.95
ISBN: 1-59337-151-9

Everything® Tween Book, $14.95
ISBN: 1-58062-870-2

Everything® Twins, Triplets, and More Book, $14.95
ISBN: 1-59337-326-0